THE OFFICIAL
JOHN WAYNE
— HANDY BOOK —
FOR BOYS

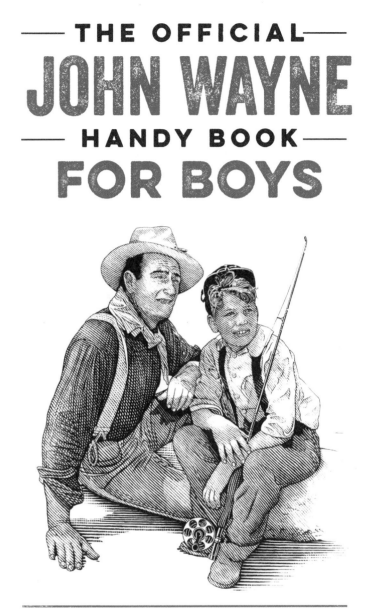

ESSENTIAL SKILLS AND FUN ACTIVITIES FOR ADVENTUROUS, SELF-RELIANT KIDS

JAMES ELLIS

ILLUSTRATIONS BY PATRICK WELSH
COVER ILLUSTRATION BY RICHARD PHIPPS

CONTENTS

John Wayne on the set of *The Fighting Kentuckian* (1949).

PAGE 170

FUN & GAMES

"NEVER THINK ANYONE IS BETTER THAN YOU, BUT NEVER ASSUME YOU'RE SUPERIOR TO ANYONE ELSE."

—JOHN WAYNE

IN ADDITION TO BEING ONE of the world's biggest movie stars, my father, John Wayne, believed in having good clean fun. A proud patriot, he would be the first to note the "pursuit of happiness" is an unalienable right listed in the Declaration of Independence, and for good reason—it's what makes life exciting. He played almost as hard as he worked—which is to say, a lot—and taught my siblings and me how to appreciate leisure activities as soon as we'd finished our chores. His enduring ethos was simple: If you're gonna take the time to do something, do it right. Our right to liberty is as much a guarantee of freedom as it is of responsibility: to make the most of our free time while we have it. Of course, all of this starts with knowing what we're doing in the first place, which takes practice.

Whether he was learning to surf in Southern California as a young man, playing chess on countless movie sets, penning letters to fans all over the world or fishing on his beloved yacht, the *Wild Goose*, my father knew these skills took time to master and delighted in honing his abilities. Better still, he took great pleasure in passing them down to us with the hope we'd grow up to be independent, respectful and kind adults, just as his father had done for him.

This spirited collection of activities is a highlight reel of the best memories boyhood has to offer, from exploring our country's natural wonders to pitching in as a member of your household. Best of all, you'll learn how to come into your own as a self-reliant adult, ready to take on the world and everything in it. Don't be surprised if you wind up giving your folks a pointer or two along the way. Saddle up and read on to discover how you can become as self-sufficient as John Wayne.

—ETHAN WAYNE

WHO WAS JOHN WAYNE?

 OU MIGHT BE WONDERING who this John Wayne person is and why he's such an expert on so many skills. It's a good question! Here's how John Wayne ("Duke" to his friends) became an American legend who embodied the spirit of independence and grit that makes our country special.

ONE OF THE FIRST THINGS to know about John Wayne is that he wasn't called "John Wayne" until he grew up. He was born Marion Robert Morrison on May 26, 1907, in a small town in Iowa.

When Marion was 7 years old, he and his family moved to Mojave, California, to live on a farm. Here Marion and his younger brother, Robert, learned a lot about self-sufficiency and grit. Marion would get up early in the morning before dawn and do his chores on the farm. Then he'd ride his pony Jenny to school, which was miles away. All of that hard work taught Marion never to give up or complain, no matter how tough things got.

One of Marion's constant companions during his childhood was an Airedale terrier called Duke. Duke followed him everywhere, and people in town would call the dog "Big Duke" and Marion "Little Duke." After a while, they just started calling Marion "Duke," and that was a nickname that would stick with him his entire life.

No matter what he was called, Marion stood out by being a great student and athlete. As a teenager, he loved playing football, and he earned a scholarship to the University of Southern California, which is in Los Angeles. Just like today, Los Angeles was the center of the movie industry and was filled with stars and celebrities. To earn money, Marion worked a job moving heavy equipment around the movie sets and was occasionally asked to act in the background to make scenes feel more realistic. One day, a movie director noticed how much the young man looked like the perfect fit for his new Western movie, *The Big Trail* (1930). The director offered Marion the lead role, and Marion accepted, changing his name to "John Wayne" for the film because it sounded more heroic to the director.

The Big Trail came out in 1930, but it didn't sell a lot of tickets. The Great Depression had just hit the country, and lots of people didn't have the money to spend at the movies. On top of that, the film required movie theaters to spend money on special equipment to show it. Because many theaters couldn't afford this equipment, they didn't show the movie. John Wayne didn't give up his dream of being an actor and kept working in Hollywood. After a time, people began recognizing his talent and hard work, and John Wayne became one of the biggest stars in the world! He mostly played cowboys or other Western heroes but also acted as a soldier in plenty of movies. No matter what the role was, people loved how John Wayne brought his sense of rugged, tough-as-nails bravery to the big screen.

John Wayne in costume on the set of *Somewhere in Sonora* (1933).

Even when he wasn't playing a sheriff bringing justice to the frontier or a soldier defending freedom around the world, John Wayne did plenty in his private life that people admired. He always took the time to answer letters from his fans and made it a point to give back to his home community of Newport Beach, California, where he lived with his wife and children. John Wayne was also one of the first celebrities to help raise awareness about cancer and the importance of getting regular check-ups from your doctor. Even more than his grit and independence, John Wayne's big heart and compassion are what made him a hero to millions of fans. He understood the value of self-sufficiency, instilling it in his children and grandchildren. Many of the lessons he taught them, as well as the values he held dear, are included in the pages of this book.

BECOME SOMEONE EVERYONE CAN COUNT ON

VER HAVE THAT SINKING feeling in your stomach when you realize you're in over your head? Maybe you had to change a tire on your bike, or you wandered off the trail on a camping trip. Feeling helpless isn't fun. The good news is that you've already taken a big step toward never feeling that way again by picking up this book!

That's because every page is chock-full of knowledge, the first thing you need to become a self-sufficient individual. You can't start building campfires (pg. 22), making perfect paper airplanes (pg. 188) or popping ollies like a pro (pg. 212) without taking the time to learn the ins and outs of the skills required. Reading the instructions is your first step, but it takes more than book learning to become self-sufficient. You also acquire knowledge through action and the ability to think critically (pg. 152), which means you'll want to set aside some time to practice these skills before you find yourself in a situation where you have to perform on the spot. And since several of these skills are potentially dangerous, be sure you have adult supervision until you learn how to do them properly.

You'll have to practice a lot—probably more than you think (and that's OK)! That's why you'll also need plenty of determination to become self-sufficient. These skills aren't easy to get the hang of—if they were, being self-sufficient wouldn't be anything special. But even if you fail the first or the 20th time at one of the tasks in this book, that's no reason to give up. All of these skills take time. As long as you're learning, you're still making progress (even if the only thing you learned is what not to do). Keep at it and your determination will be rewarded.

John Wayne as Breck Coleman in *The Big Trail* (1930).

The bumps along the road to self-sufficiency should teach you humility, which is important! Humility means you recognize you aren't perfect and that there's always room to improve. A humble person is someone who is always ready to learn and grow. Humility should also remind you to be patient and kind to others who don't have your skills and inspire you to pass along your knowledge. That way, you're not only helping yourself, you're also helping make the world a better place!

DUKE'S DOs AND DON'Ts

 O BE THE BEST version of yourself possible, keep things simple: There's stuff you should do, and stuff you shouldn't. Keep these helpful tips in mind as you read, pilgrim!

FOR OUTDOOR SKILLS

Do

• Make sure to carry a compass with you when you head out on a hike. Although you can find true north using other methods, nothing is easier than having a compass!

• Leave your campsite in better condition than you found it. Never leave behind litter, and, if you're able, take a moment to clean up trash or debris others might have left behind.

• Get permission from your folks before heading out on any hike or camping trip. And make sure to let a friend or family member know your destination and path when you leave home. If you and your group get lost, this person can help find you!

• Bring more food and water with you on a camping trip than you think you'll need. It's also a good idea to bring a small first aid kit to deal with any cuts, scrapes or bug bites.

Don't

• Leave a fire unattended, even if it seems small.

• Eat any plants or fruit in the wild you can't 100 percent identify as safe.

• Go swimming (either in a pool or lake or the ocean) by yourself. Always bring a buddy! Always check for signs that confirm if swimming is allowed and safe.

• Take a drink of salt water when swimming in the ocean. It's bad for you!

FOR SELF-SUFFICIENCY AT HOME

Do

• Pick up after yourself at home. If you see a mess, take a moment to clean it up.

• Ask your parents if there are any chores you can do around the house. You'll earn their respect and feel good about doing your part, too!

• Check your house's smoke detectors once a month to make sure they're working.

Don't

• Run around inside the house. It's not only dangerous, but it's also disrespectful to everyone else. If you want to run, go outside!

• Play with scissors, knives or anything else that can cut you without either knowing what you're doing or having an adult around.

• Forget to say "please" and "thank you." Mind your manners!

John Wayne in *The Fighting Kentuckian* (1949).

FOR ACTING UPWARDS

Do

- Try to do something new every once in a while. You need to shake things up now and again. That's how you grow.

- Take the time to write thank-you notes whenever you receive a gift or someone does you a good turn.

- Make sure you treat others the way you'd like them to treat you (that should always start with respect).

Don't

- Judge people by how they look or where they're from—it's how they act that counts.

- Just wait for your turn to talk when in a conversation—really listen to what the other person is saying.

- Talk about anything that happens in the bathroom when in public. Trust us: It isn't as funny as you think.

FOR FUN & GAMES

Do

- Keep a variety of games at home—from a deck of cards to a checker or chess board to board games—so that you can stave off boredom and find something to play that everyone likes.

- Take the time to explain the rules of a game to someone who has never played before. And be patient!

- Play fair and by the rules; otherwise, you're just cheating yourself.

Don't

- Be a sore winner or loser. If you win, don't brag about it. If you lose, don't whine. Either way, keep your chin up.

- Get discouraged if your game or activity doesn't turn out perfect—it's about the fun you have along the way, not the destination.

- Be afraid to try new games. Variety is the spice of life!

John Wayne on the set of *Donovan's Reef* (1963).

OUTDOOR SKILLS

ROUGH IT WITH CONFIDENCE WHENEVER YOU VENTURE OUT INTO THE WILD FRONTIER

HOW TO MANEUVER A CANOE

EOPLE HAVE used canoes for thousands of years to travel through the water. Now it's your turn! Here are some pointers on how to steer one.

1. GET READY TO PADDLE

While experienced canoers can paddle on their own, most people find it helpful to team up with a partner (in your case, it should be an adult you trust). You and your partner should each pick a different side of the canoe to paddle on—left or right. The person responsible for steering the canoe should sit near the stern (that's the back of the canoe) while their partner sits near the bow (front).

Make sure to wear a life vest!

2. HOLD TIGHT

Grab the top of your paddle with your "inside" hand, or the hand farthest away from the side of the canoe you're paddling on. If you're paddling on the right side of the canoe, grab the top of the paddle with your left hand. Make sure your left hand completely covers the grip on the top of the paddle, with your thumb pointed parallel to the water. Next, place your right hand right above where the shaft of the paddle meets the blade (the flat part at the end).

3. SMOOTH AND STEADY

To go forward, stretch the paddle forward, then dip the entire blade into the water in front of you. Next, keeping the blade underwater, twist your upper body until you've dragged the paddle behind you, then lift the paddle out of the water and bring it forward to take your next stroke. The four images to the right illustrate the action of one full stroke from start to finish. When paddling with a partner, stroke together at the same time to go in a straight line.

4. GENTLE TURNS

If you're in the back and want to turn the canoe, tell the partner up front to stop paddling. If you want to steer right, start paddling on the right side of the canoe until you're happy with where you're heading, and tell your partner to resume paddling on the opposite side so the canoe stops turning. Want to go left? Do the same thing, except you paddle on the left side of the canoe.

5. *SLOWING IT DOWN*

You and your partner should place your paddles vertically in the water (blade first, perpendicular to the side of the canoe) and hold them there until you've slowed down. Remember, it's better to be safe than sorry when it comes to setting your speed.

HOW TO TELL TIME WITHOUT A WATCH

HEN YOU'RE traveling through the great outdoors, it's important to know how much daylight you have left so you have plenty of time to get somewhere safe for the night. Here are some ways to know the time of day without depending on any devices.

1. TOUCH THE SUN

Find somewhere that gives you a clear view of the horizon and the sun in the sky; otherwise, this technique won't work. Stretch out one arm with your hand turned sideways, palm facing you. Your fingers should be stacked on top of each other without any space between them.

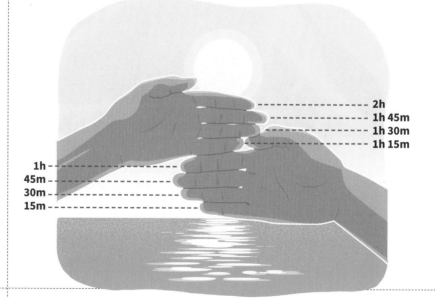

Now position your hand so your index finger (that's the long one closest to your thumb) lines up with the sun's bottom in the sky. Next, count how many fingers "fit" between the sun's bottom and where the land off in the horizon begins. Each finger represents about 15 minutes. If you can only fit two fingers in the space between the sun and the horizon, that means you only have 30 minutes until dark. If all four fingers fit and you still have room, however, you can hold up your other hand (palm facing you) and stack it below your first hand. Now you have eight fingers to work with!

2. STICK TO IT

If you're looking for another way to tell time in the wilderness and have some patience, you can use a stick and a sunny patch of ground. Find a spot on the ground that gets constant sunlight and, at

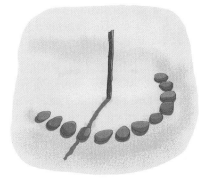

dawn, plant a stick upright. The shadow of the stick will shrink as noon approaches and lengthen as the sun sets.

Throughout the day, use stones or anything else handy to mark where the shadow is as it changes locations. At the end of the first day, you should have a semicircle of markers that trace the path of the shadow and sun. Depending on the season, you have roughly 10–14 hours of daylight (10 in winter, 12 in autumn and spring and 14 during summer).

Take a look at your semicircle of markers. While leaving the markers at each end of the semicircle alone, rearrange the other markers so they are evenly spaced out based on the hours of daylight you have each day. So if it's spring, for example, and you have 12 hours of daylight, make sure your semicircle is made up of 12 markers. Each time the shadow of the stick moves from one marker to the next, that means one hour has passed.

HOW TO BUILD AND TEND A FIRE

HO'S AFRAID of the dark? Not you, once you learn how to start a rip-roaring fire that's perfect for your next night out in the wilderness.

1. *PLAN AHEAD AND PICK YOUR SITE*

Like most things worth doing, building a fire takes a little time and patience. That means you don't want to get started when you're just a few minutes from sundown. Find a suitable site for your fire—someplace dry and sheltered from the wind, but not covered in dry grass or leaves—at least an hour before you need to light things up.

2. *GATHER YOUR MATERIALS*

You'll want extra wood on hand to keep the fire going.

Fuel

This is what you call your larger pieces of wood—the biggest of branches or small, dry logs—that you'll feed the fire throughout the night.

Kindling

Bigger branches, like the kind you might find at the base of the tree, will feed your fire without being so large as to snuff it out.

Tinder

Look for dry, lightweight materials such as twigs, dry grass and wood shavings that can easily ignite.

Build on clear, dry ground at least 6 feet from any trees, bushes and grass.

3. *PUT IT ALL TOGETHER*

Now that you have almost everything you need, it's time to build your fire. Place your kindling in an area that's clear of dead grass or flammable plants—you don't want your fire to burn out of control!

Place your tinder in between and around the kindling, which you can stack in a teepee shape like the one on the previous page. Once you light the tinder, the flame should be protected from the wind and will turn into a cozy fire in no time.

4. *ASK FOR A LIGHT*

Let a responsible adult handle setting the fire. You have a much more important job, which is to make sure it keeps burning in a controlled way! As the fire burns and begins to die down, take one of the bigger, thicker pieces of wood you gathered for fuel and add it to the fire. The thicker and dryer the fuel, the longer and better it will burn.

Be sure to keep some distance from the heat and the smoke.

5. *PAY ATTENTION*
Gathering around a campfire is a real treat and a good reminder of why we love the great outdoors, but fire isn't a toy. Respect the danger an out-of-control fire can be—never leave a fire unattended or go to sleep with it still burning, and keep plenty of water and a shovel handy so you can put out any ornery flames. If the campfire starts burning outside the area you have built for it, toss water and shovel dirt on it to kill it. Better the fire than you, pilgrim.

THINGS TO DO AROUND A CAMPFIRE
Nothing beats sitting by the fire in the great outdoors. Grab your friends and try all of these fireside favorites.

Sing Songs
Belt out your favorite tunes or take turns creating something new!

Tell Scary Stories
The scarier the better. Make up some spine-tingling tales (or throw in some real ones!) and see who you can manage to spook.

Make S'mores
The ultimate fireside treat! Roast marshmallows until they're golden brown, then sandwich them with chocolate in between two graham crackers and go to town. Just be sure to make extra!

Cook Dinner
Serve up meals like a real cowboy. With an adult's help, roast your food over an open fire and dig in like John Wayne (see pg. 40).

HOW TO WORK WITH FIRE SAFELY

OW THAT YOU know the basics of building a fire to keep you warm and cozy, learn about how to work with it like a real pro.

1. *TIMING YOUR FIREWOOD*

Wondering how long that branch you just threw onto the fire will last before you have to feed the flames again? In general, "hardwood," which usually comes from trees with leaves that fall off in the autumn, will be tougher to ignite but burns long. "Softwood" is usually from pine trees that have cones. This kind of wood tends to catch fire easily but it also burns quickly. If you're looking to keep the fire going for a while, try to find some hardwood. And be sure to gather up as much as you can—it's always better to have too much on hand than not enough!

2. *DON'T ROCK OUT*

While some people add rocks to their fire to help with cooking, you should never do this. No matter how solid a rock looks on the outside, most of them have little hollow pockets on their insides that sometimes contain water. When heated in the fire, the water expands and the rocks can explode, which can be very dangerous! On the right, Duke's illustrating what you should NOT do.

Duke in *A Lady Takes a Chance* (1943).

3. *PUT IT OUT LIKE A PRO*

When you're done with your fire, you want to make sure it stays done with you. Take your bucket of water (which you should always have nearby when tending a fire) and pour it on the flames, putting them out. Then stir the smoldering ashes with a stick and pour some more water over the pile just to make sure. If anything still smokes or you can spot any embers, keep adding water until it's a cold pile of ash.

HOW TO BUILD A SHELTER

OTHING SHOWS OFF your survival skills better than making your own shelter out of whatever Mother Nature provides. Here are some basic types you and an adult can try to create next time you're in the outdoors.

1. *SAFETY FIRST WHEN SELECTING*
Before you start building a shelter, you need to put some thought into where you want to hunker down for the night. As a general rule, you want to avoid ground that's wet or damp for obvious comfort reasons (Who wants to go to sleep in wet mud?). But you should also avoid valleys or ditches in case of flooding from a sudden rainstorm. And you also want to stay away from any dead trees or trees with loose-looking branches that could fall and hit you if the wind picks up.

It might not be big, but you should fit comfortably in your shelter.

2. THE LEAN-TO

Setting up this shelter should be a piece of cake for even the most inexperienced camper, but it requires having a fallen tree, large rock face or something similar at your campsite. If you have a suitable object you can lean branches against, your next step is simple: gather long branches and lean them side-by-side against the object so you create a space just large enough to fit your body. Cover the outside of the branches with leaves, soil or anything else to create a thick wall that will help trap heat in your shelter. Now you just have to crawl in and relax!

3. *THE A-FRAME*

If you don't have any nearby objects that can help with a lean-to shelter, you can try to build the A-frame. First, find a long branch (around 12 feet if one's around) and two shorter branches (about half the length of the long branch). Push one end of each shorter branch into the ground, so that they're sticking up parallel to one another, with room enough for you to fit between, and lean the top of the branches together so they touch. Then take the long branch and place it at the top of where the two smaller branches touch so that all three branches look like an "A" when looking at them head-on.

Take some twine (if you don't have twine, you can use your shoelaces, your belt or even any grass that looks strong enough to hold a knot if you're short on options) and tie all three branches together where they meet. Now that you have an A-frame, get at least six or seven other branches to lean side-by-side against each side of the longer branch. Cover this frame with leaves, grass and other materials that can help keep you warm. That's it!

4. THE EMERGENCY DEBRIS SHELTER

If you want to upgrade your A-frame to a cozier shelter, take some smaller, flexible branches and twigs and "weave" them between the branches making up the sides of your shelter. Now take any nearby debris and pile it on the top and sides of your shelter until you have 2-3 feet of thickness all around. After you're done, lay some sticks on the outside of the debris to help prevent the wind from ruining your snug home for the night!

HOW TO HANG A BEAR BAG

WHEN CAMPING, it's best to remember you're not the only one in the woods who's hungry. To avoid attracting critters looking for a midnight snack, you need to hang food (and other supplies that have a strong smell) from a tree before turning in for the night.

1. *THE SUPPLIES YOU'LL NEED*
Before heading out for your camping trip, check with an adult to make sure you're bringing the following:

1 NYLON BAG
that can
fit all of
your waste,
foodstuff and
more (many
camping
supply stores
sell bags
specifically
to hang
from a tree)

1 ROPE
about 100
feet long

1 CARABINER
(a special
metal loop
you can also
buy at most
camping
supply stores)

**1 ONE-POUND
BARBELL**
(just in case
you can't find
a heavy rock,
which you'll
need later)

2. *GATHER EVERYTHING TOGETHER*
Collect anything a wild animal might consider food from your campsite. Beyond obvious items such as leftover hot dogs and other snacks, this means collecting trash, toothpaste, sunblock and more—anything that gives off a strong smell.

3. *BAG IT UP*
Place everything you've gathered in the nylon bag. Tie it shut and grab an adult to help with the next steps.

4. *FIND YOUR TREES*
Find a pair of tall trees about 200 feet away from your campsite. The trees should be at least 15 feet tall and 20 feet away from each other. They also need thick, heavy branches that will support the weight of your bag.

5. *HANG YOUR ROPE*

Tie one end of the rope you brought to either the barbell or a nearby heavy rock—whichever is easiest! Tie the other end of the rope around the trunk of one of the trees. Let's call this Tree #1. Next, either you or your adult should throw the end of the rope tied to your rock/barbell over a branch of Tree #1. Watch out to make sure it doesn't hit you or anyone else on the way down! Collect the end of the rope, walk to the second tree and throw the rope over a branch on Tree #2. Your rope should be draped over two branches on two separate trees, with enough slack so it sags in the middle.

6. *HANG THE BAG*

In the middle of the rope where it's sagging, tie a loop with that part of the rope. Take the carabiner, attach it to your bag, then use it to attach the bag to the loop.

7. RAISE THE BAG

At the free end of the rope (the one tied to a rock or weight), untie the rope from the rock or weight and pull on the rope to hoist your bag at least 12 feet off the ground. Once the bag is out of reach, tie the end of the rope you're holding around the trunk of Tree #2. Try to make sure the loop around the tree is tied off just below a branch or prominent knot so the loop doesn't slip up the trunk of the tree in the night and bring your bag lower to the ground where a bear or other wild animal can get at it. Now your bag is safe from bears and other wild animals.

HOW TO FIND TRUE NORTH

 NE OF THE quickest ways to tell a tenderfoot from a trailhand is if they can find their way in the wilderness. Learn how to find true north in almost any situation so you're always staying on the right track.

1. USING A COMPASS

Having the right tools for the job always makes life a little easier, and a compass will have you pointed in the right direction in no time! Because the needle of the compass has been magnetized, it will always point north no matter how you hold it. Still, the best way to hold the compass is face up in front of you, with the N pointing away from you. Then turn your body until the colored tip of the needle lines up with the N on top of the compass. Good job, you're now facing north!

2. *CHECK THE SUN*
If you find yourself without a compass, you can still find north by relying on the sun. The sun always rises in the east and sets in the west. If it's the morning or late afternoon, you can find east or west by spotting where the sun is in the sky. Once you have your bearings, finding north is simply a matter of turning 90 degrees left (if you're facing east) or 90 degrees right (if you're facing west).

3. *THE SHADOW METHOD*
Using the sun to orient yourself can be tricky in the middle of the day when it's above your head. With a little patience, though, you can still find north. Find a spot on the ground with plenty of direct sunlight. Place a stick upright in the ground and use a rock or other object to mark the tip of its shadow. Wait 15 to 20 minutes, and mark where the tip of the shadow has moved with another rock. The shadow will have moved from west to east. If you stand between the shadows with the first mark on your left, you are facing north.

TIP
You might've heard moss grows on the northern side of trees, but that's not always true. Turns out, moss grows wherever it's damp, so carry a compass instead.

HOW TO REPEL MOSQUITOES

 HESE BLOODSUCKERS are more than just annoying pests—they are also potential carriers of diseases ranging from the annoying to the deadly. Here's how you can enjoy nature without also becoming a buffet for bugs.

1. *COVER UP*

Wear clothing that covers as much skin as possible without being cumbersome. You want to use common sense here—wearing a parka would provide excellent protection

An adult can help you spray any hard-to-reach areas.

against mosquitoes but probably isn't practical for a hot summer day. A long-sleeved shirt, pants and socks that pull up to your shins will do. Mosquitoes can easily spot both dark and bright, bold colors, so you should dress in light colors (think white or beige) when possible.

2. GET YOUR SPRAY ON
It takes a lot to deter a mosquito from attacking you. To them, you're basically a giant $5 milkshake they can sip on for free. But one surefire way to make yourself disgusting (to the mosquitoes at least) is by applying mosquito repellent.

There are many different types of repellent, but you can sort them into two categories—those containing a chemical called DEET and those without. Those with DEET will repel mosquitoes the longest (up to five hours in some cases), but you can only apply them once per day. You can apply repellent made of natural ingredients (such as oil of lemon eucalyptus) multiple times per day (and you'll probably have to, since it doesn't last as long as repellent with DEET).

No matter what type you choose, keep it away from your eyes, nose and mouth and don't apply it on any part of your skin that's broken (like with a cut or scrape) or sunburned.

3. SMOKE 'EM OUT
After a long day of hiking, the last thing you want to deal with is a swarm of hungry mosquitoes. Build a fire (see pg. 22) and make sure to occasionally feed it with branches containing green leaves. This will cause your fire to produce more smoke, which helps keep insects away.

HOW TO COOK WITH AN OPEN FLAME

 OU CAN ONLY live on hot dogs and s'mores for so long. Learn how to cook up something tastier on the trail using a campfire.

1. *COOK WITH THE FIRE, NOT ON IT*
Before we explore what kind of tools you need to cook with an open flame, it's important to point out you're not going to get a good result by sticking food directly into an open flame. When fire directly touches your food, it will almost always burn the outside to a crisp while leaving the inside of your food uncooked. Fortunately, there's a better way to use your fire's heat to make your next meal.

John Wayne and Syd Saylor in *Born to the West* (1937).

2. GET A STEW GOING

For a simple and delicious meal when camping, it's tough to beat a stew. All you need is a cooking pot, some clean drinking water and something to cook (and a little patience). Maybe you've gone fishing or hunting that day, or maybe you've brought food with you from home. Either way, cooking your food in a pot lets fat and other flavors stay in the pot and not drip into the fire. Ask an adult to rake some hot coals out of the fire so that they're near the flame without being in it. Then place your pot full of food in the nest of coals, sit back and wait until your meal is done.

3. WRAP IT UP

You can also wrap your food in layers of tinfoil. Once the foil completely covers the food, you can place the package directly in the hot coals (for potatoes) or over the hot coals (similar to what you do with a pot when making stew) for corn.

Corn

Potatoes

HOW TO BUILD A SNOW SHELTER

IF YOU'RE STRANDED in a wintry wasteland, knowing how to build a snow shelter could save your life. It's also fun. The next time it snows, build a cozy cave in your backyard and see for yourself. Have an adult nearby, just in case it collapses on you!

1. *PILE IT ON*

If you see a nearby snowbank (a big mound of snow already created) you can skip this step. If not, create your own pile by gathering nearby snow into a mound about 4 feet high. Make sure it's wide enough that your whole body will fit inside it. Just like when you're building a snowman, you want to find snow that's wet enough to pack but not so wet that it's slush.

2. *DIG IT*

Get ready to work up a sweat with all of the digging you have ahead of you. Create a door by digging a hole in the snow mound big enough for you to crawl through. This

should be at the base of the mound. Crawl in and start digging upward toward the top of the mound. This ensures you can create an elevated space for yourself inside the mound that will help trap your body heat.

3. *PATCH IT UP*

While hollowing out the mound, you might accidentally break through one of the "walls" of your shelter. Don't panic—you can fix it. After you finish digging the living space in the shelter, pop outside and gather more snow to patch up any holes so that everything is sealed. The walls should be at least 1 foot thick.

HOW TO RECOGNIZE DEADLY SNAKES

S **EE SOMETHING** slithering ahead of you on the trail? It's best to keep your distance. But if you're curious and give the snake plenty of room, you might be able to spot whether or not it's venomous.

1. USE THEIR HEAD

As a general rule, most venomous snakes have heads that look more like a triangle (but not always, as you can see with the coral snake). If the snake has a flattened, pointy head, then you might want to be even more careful than usual.

2. LISTEN FOR DANGER

One telltale signal of a (potentially) deadly snake is the sound of a rattle. Most species of rattlesnake—one of the most dangerous kinds of snake in the U.S.—will shake the rattles at the end of their tails as a warning that they're not to be trifled with. But just because you don't hear anything doesn't mean a snake can't harm you. There are more species of deadly snakes than just the rattlesnake, and some species of rattlesnake don't even have a rattle!

Rattlesnake

Copperhead Snakes

3. CHECK THE COLORS

Many snakes, like the rattlesnake, have colors that blend into their environment. Snakes like the coral snake, however, signify their venomous nature with their brightly colored skins. Get to know the colors of the venomous snakes in any area you may be traveling through.

Coral Snake

HOW TO RECOGNIZE POISONOUS PLANTS

HE OUTDOORS offers access to plenty of beautiful flowers and plants, but not all of them are safe to touch. Learn how to spot some of the most poisonous plants you're likely to encounter on the trail.

1. COUNT THE LEAVES

Three of the most common poisonous plants in the United States are poison ivy, poison oak and poison sumac. Unfortunately, they also look like most other green, leafy plants at a glance. You'll have to pay closer attention and count the number of leaves a plant has on each stem to help determine if it's poisonous. Poison ivy usually has three broad leaves, each shaped like a tear drop. Poison oak will also have three leaves, but they look more like the leaves of an oak tree. Poison sumac might have anything from seven to 13 leaves with smooth edges per stem.

2. SHINY MEANS DANGER (MAYBE)

If a plant's leaves look wet or oily, you don't want to touch it. While an oily-looking leaf isn't always dangerous, in some cases it means it is covered in poison that can irritate your skin.

Poison Oak

Poison Ivy

BE BERRY CAREFUL

Never ever eat any berries you find outdoors, even if they look like the kind you see in the grocery store. Many can make you sick, or worse!

Poison Sumac

HOW TO RAISE YOUR BODY TEMPERATURE

 OU NEED TO keep warm when heading out on a chilly day, but that's easier said than done when you're already outside. Here are some tips to stay toasty when on the go.

1. *LAYER UP*

Depending on how cold it is outside, you'll want to dress in multiple layers. Start with long underwear and pile on the clothes from there. You want plenty of layers to trap your body heat and keep you cozy.

2. *TAKE SHELTER*

When it's too cold outside, the best solution is to head indoors! Of course, when you're in the middle of the woods, finding a warm room inside isn't always possible. But you can still stay warm by making a temporary shelter (check out pg. 28) from the cold. Just remember your shelter needs to keep you dry and out of the wind.

3. *FIRE IT UP*

If you're planning on staying in one place and you already know how to start a fire, you can take the time to build one to beat back the cold. This will take some time, so if you're really feeling the chill, this isn't the best way to keep yourself warm—especially if you haven't built a fire before and might struggle to put one together. To learn more about building a fire, see pg. 22.

John Wayne in *Island in the Sky* (1953), a survival film that takes place in the frozen wilderness of Canada.

HOW TO SAFELY CARVE USING A KNIFE

 UT ON THE TRAIL, a good knife can help you craft the tools that will help you survive the wilderness. But you need to learn how to handle one safely so you don't harm yourself or others.

1. *STAY SHARP*
Make sure the knife you're working with is up to snuff—you want the blade to be plenty sharp so you don't have to use too much force when carving. Otherwise, you risk losing control and harming yourself.

2. *TAKE A SEAT*
Anytime you're working with a knife, it's serious business. Find a quiet place where you can sit down and concentrate on the task at hand. Sitting down also helps keep you more stable as you carve and gives you more control of your motions.

3. *GET A GRIP*
Take the knife in your dominant hand and wrap your fingers around the handle, placing your thumb on top of the handle. Make

sure the blade—that's the sharp part of the knife—faces away from you. Now grab the wood you're going to carve in your other hand and get ready to start working.

4. OUT AND AWAY
Hold both the knife and the wood away from your body. You don't need to stretch out your arms unnaturally, but it's important to make sure that you're carving into empty space and not into your leg. When carving, always move the knife away from you in a controlled, smooth motion. Keeping the blade at a 45-degree angle to the wood will help you carve efficiently and safely.

5. CREATE A SAFE SPACE
Make sure anyone with you keeps at least an arm's length away while you are carving. That way, if the knife slips, you can avoid hurting them.

HOW TO SHARPEN A KNIFE

SHARP KNIFE is a safe knife, so learn how to keep the edge of your blade in tip-top condition.

1. TEST FOR SHARPNESS

Before you get to work sharpening your knife, you should check to make sure it's actually dull. The safest method is to shine a flashlight on the edge of the knife. An edge that's dull is flat compared to a sharp one and will reflect light back at you. So if you see a light on the edge, it's time to sharpen the knife!

2. ROCK OUT

The best way to sharpen a knife is using a whetstone, a special type of rock specifically made for just this purpose. But if you don't have one and need to sharpen your knife right now, take a look at the rocks around you. A rock with a flat, mostly smooth surface (that still has a little grit) will serve in a pinch.

Whetstone

Hunting Knife

Be very mindful of where your fingers are on the blade.

3. GET TO WORK

Once you have your stone, place it on a flat surface. Now grab your knife by its handle with one hand and place your other hand on the flat side of the blade. Be very careful not to cut yourself on the edge! Place the knife's edge flat on one end of the stone closest to you and then raise the blade so it's at a shallow angle with the stone while the edge is still making contact. Slide the blade away from you down the stone, making sure the edge maintains contact, until you reach the far end of the stone. Now flip the blade and do the same thing in the other direction. Repeat until you have a sharp knife again!

HOW TO TREAD WATER

OOLING OFF in a swimming pool or lake can be a fun way to spend an afternoon, but you'll have an even better time if you know how to tread water. Learn how to stay in place in the water so you can stay safe and keep playing. Until you've mastered the technique, make sure to practice with an adult nearby.

1. *SLOW AND STEADY*
One of the most important parts of treading water is to keep the motions of your arms and legs in a steady rhythm. You're trying to save energy, so be mindful as opposed to frantic with your movement.

2. *STRAIGHT LEGS AND CIRCLES*
2A. Keep your legs and feet pointing straight down and kick back and forth. At the same time, you should be making large, circular motions with your arms underwater. How? 2B. First, stretch your arms out in front of you, then separate your arms with the palms facing outwards as if you were trying to push the water out to your sides. Finally, bring your arms back so they are together in front of you.

3. *LEAN BACK*
If you're getting tired of treading water, try changing things up by floating on your back. Once you're on your back, keep your arms and legs underwater and bend your arms at their elbows. Paddle your hands and kick your feet up and down (remember, slow and steady!) to stay afloat while giving your core a bit of a breather.

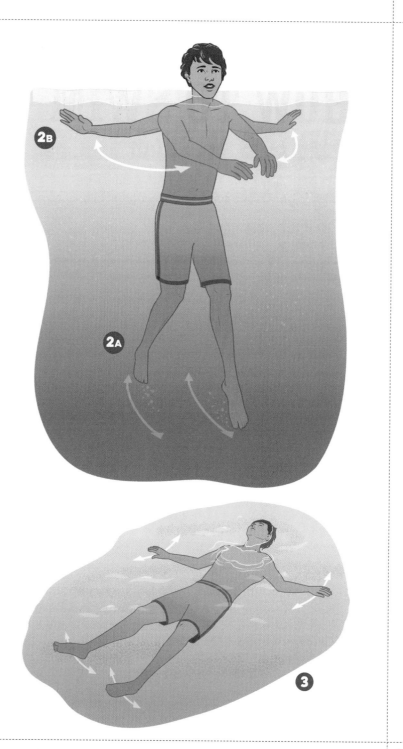

HOW TO SWIM

 OU'RE MISSING OUT on some of the best fun the outdoors has to offer if you can't swim! If you need to learn how to swim, follow the steps below, but make sure to do so with the help of an adult.

1. *GO WITH THE FLOW*
Swimming is all about controlling your movement through the water. Before you start worrying about learning different strokes, you need to make sure you approach swimming with a relaxed attitude. You're here to have fun!

2. *KEEP COORDINATED*
The difference between swimming gracefully through the water and sinking like a stone can boil down to coordination. Your legs and arms work together to keep you moving without exhausting you too quickly. In general, smooth arm and leg movements beat out short, jerky motions.

3. *REMEMBER TO BREATHE*
It takes effort to swim, so you'll have to pace your breathing to avoid getting winded. Depending on the style of swimming, it's a good idea to take a breath every other stroke. And you should practice exhaling while your face is still underwater. That way, when you raise your face out of the water while swimming, you don't waste any time in taking in a big breath of air.

4. *CRAWL THROUGH THE WATER*
Beginner swimmers like you can start with the freestyle stroke. It's also called the front crawl stroke because it will look like you're crawling on your hands when swimming. Here's how to swim the freestyle:
    4A. Float on your stomach and stretch out one of your arms. Keep your fingers together and slightly bent so you're clawing at the water ahead of you.
    4B. Once you've stretched your arm as far as you can, drag it back to your side while keeping it underwater. While doing

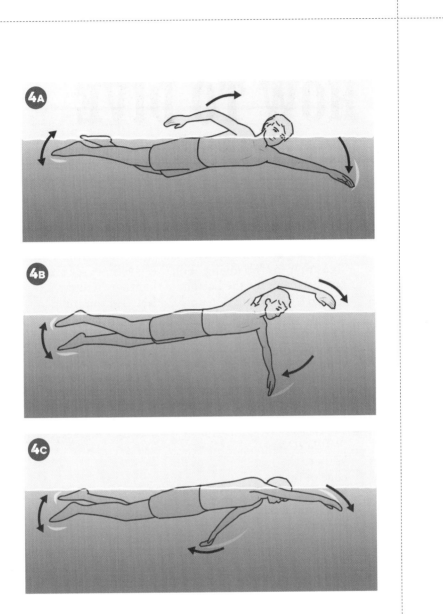

that, stretch out your other arm to perform the same stroke. 4C. While you perform the strokes with your arms, your legs should be kept together as much as you can while you kick your feet up and down at a steady pace. Don't bend your knees too much. This is called a flutter kick and will provide you with another source of momentum. Congratulations! You're swimming freestyle.

HOW TO DIVE

TOP BELLY FLOPPING into the water and learn how to safely enter the water with grace and style. Swimming is a lot more fun when you don't have a sore stomach.

1. *MAKE SURE IT'S SAFE*
The first rule when diving is to only do it where you're absolutely certain the water is deep enough. If you see signs that say "no diving," don't. If you don't see signs but also can't see the bottom of the water, assume it's too shallow and don't dive, otherwise you could seriously injure yourself. In general, you want the water to be at least 8 feet deep.

2. *ASSUME THE POSITION*
Walk to the edge of the water and stand with your knees slightly bent. Your dominant foot should be about a step in front of your other foot.

3. TAKE AIM

Bend down at your waist until your upper body is parallel to the ground. Stretch your arms forward and point your hands at the water so your arms form a triangle with your head at the bottom. You want to keep your chin tucked down against your chest and your biceps pressed against your ears.

4. DIVE!

Now push forward hard with both feet to launch yourself at an angle toward the water. Try to keep your body relaxed and you should slide right in without causing a big splash.

HOW TO TREAT A BURN

 HEN LIFE BRINGS the heat, here's how you can take care of yourself. Even some of the most careful folks around suffer the consequences of being too close to a flame every once in a while.

1. GET IN THE CLEAR

Depending on where you've gotten burned, the affected area might be covered by clothing or a watch or some other item of jewelry. Remove it so you can get a good look at the burn, and because the hurt skin will likely swell up, making it harder (and painful!) for you to take anything off later.

2. KEEP COOL (NOT COLD)

Your first instinct after suffering a burn may be to plunge the injured area into a bucket of ice-cold water, but you'd only be half right. Definitely cool the area down by running it under cool tap water or something similar for 15 to 30 minutes. But you want to avoid ice-cold water, as that can further damage the tender tissue.

3. TAKE A LOOK

As nasty as it can be, take a look at the burned area. Is it covered in blisters that aren't broken? In that case, don't touch them and go find an adult if you haven't already. If your skin looks wet and you have gauze or non-sticky bandages on hand, gently wrap the damaged skin to protect it from infection. Then go find an adult and let them take care of it from there.

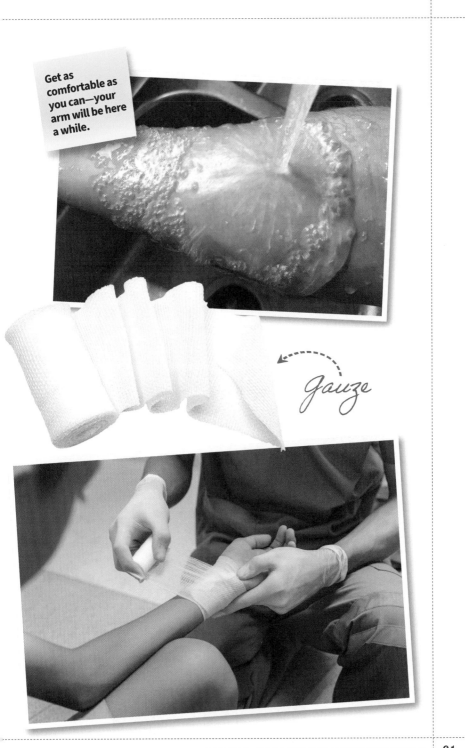

Get as comfortable as you can—your arm will be here a while.

gauze

HOW TO TREAT FROSTBITE

ROSTBITE HAPPENS when parts of your body actually freeze from exposure to extreme cold, which can have disastrous long-term consequences. It is, in other words, not cool.

1. *DON'T GET FROSTBITE IN THE FIRST PLACE*

This is a cheat, but it can't be stressed enough how important it is to protect your extremities (those are the parts of you farthest away from your heart, such as your fingers, toes, ears and nose) when going out in the cold. Wear a scarf, hat, mittens and thick socks. Preventing frostbite helps avoid the pain it can lead to.

2. *COLOR CODING*

Take a look at the part of your body you think is frostbitten. Is your skin red and painful? That's great! It means the cold hasn't damaged too much of your

When out in the elements, keep as much of your face covered as you can.

BUNDLE UP, PILGRIM!
These items will help keep frostbite at bay.

Mittens

Thermal Socks

Hat

Mask

Coat

Thermal Pants

skin yet. You can treat it by covering the cold skin and getting to someplace warm, pronto. But if the skin is gray or white or blue, then you need to see a doctor. Don't try to warm it up yourself—when it's this frozen, it needs to be treated by a professional who knows how to help without further damaging your skin.

3. *DON'T BURN YOURSELF*
If you find a source of heat, you might feel tempted to bring the frozen bits of your body as close to that source as possible. But remember, you can still burn yourself, and you don't want to deal with frostbite damage and burn damage at the same time. Keep a distance from the heat so it's keeping you warm but not making things worse.

HOW TO STOP BLEEDING

UCH! HERE'S HOW to patch up small cuts if you've nicked yourself on something sharp. Remember to find an adult so they can make sure everything's OK!

1. *KEEP IT CLEAN*
If you can get to someplace with soap and clean water, use both to gently wash the wound. Your goal here is to wash out any germs that could cause an infection. Remember not to scrub too hard—you don't want to further damage the wound.

Soap

An adult can help you apply the bandage properly.

2. PATCH IT UP WITH PRESSURE

After you clean the cut, use a bandage to wrap it up and apply firm pressure to help stop the bleeding. About five to 10 minutes of constant pressure should stop most wounds.

3. CHANGE AS NECESSARY

You're all patched up, but that doesn't mean you can ignore your wound. If your bandage gets soiled or dirty, you need to change it for a new one. This will help you avoid infection, which can lead to more serious (and painful) issues.

Bandages

HOW TO SURVIVE FALLING INTO ICY WATER

 SLIPPING INTO freezing water plunges you into a life-or-death situation, but it's manageable if you know what you need to do. Here's how you can make sure you live to swim another day.

1. *HOLD YOUR BREATH*
You might think that not breathing underwater is an obvious piece of advice you don't need, but you'd be wrong. When your body gets submerged in icy water, the shock of it often causes fast, nearly uncontrollable breathing called hyperventilation. Fight against this urge to breathe in a lungful of frigid water!

Keep your head and arms out of the water as much as possible.

2. GET OUT FAST

With the temperature of the water that cold, you'll only have a few minutes before your muscles stop working. Use that time to find the hole you fell through and place as much of your upper body through that hole as possible. Kick your feet underwater while pulling yourself out of the water to give yourself the best chance of making it out.

3. ROLL TO SAFETY

Getting out of the water is incredibly important, but don't risk trying to stand on your feet—for one, you're likely to have trouble doing so after your ice bath. More importantly, if you try to stand on ice, the pressure of your body weight might cause you to break a new hole and fall in the water again. Roll to firmer ground before standing up.

4. GET DRY

Your wet clothes now pose the biggest danger to your health. Quickly take them off and find shelter...preferably someplace with a source of heat. Tuck your knees up to your chest and cross your arms to try to preserve every bit of body heat.

Blankets and a hot beverage will help your body recover from the cold.

HOW TO SURVIVE A TORNADO

NE OF MOTHER NATURE'S most unpredictable creations, tornadoes are also surprisingly common. Here's how to keep yourself safe if a twister touches down in your area.

1. *HEED THE WARNINGS*

While tornados can sometimes form quickly and take everyone by surprise, meteorologists can usually give a heads up if current weather conditions are likely to create one of these violent windstorms. They'll issue a "tornado watch" on TV, radio and probably on your phone (or your parents' phones). This is a good time to find an adult and ask them what to do to prepare for a possible tornado.

If meteorologists spot a tornado in the area, they'll upgrade the "tornado watch" to a "tornado warning." That means you and your family should seek shelter immediately until you hear the all-clear.

Warning Horn

Don't try to outrun a tornado—find cover and stay put.

2. DIG IN

A tornado can generate winds up to 300 miles per hour, which means logs, rocks, downed trees and other debris can turn into deadly objects. If possible, you should seek shelter in the basement of a building long before the tornado touches down. But if you're caught in the open, you need to find a ditch or gully or someplace similarly low. It may be less than ideal and pretty scary, but the most important thing to keep in mind is that it's your safest option available.

3. PROTECT YOUR NECK

The biggest danger you face during a tornado isn't getting sucked up by the storm (which is definitely bad but also rare), it's getting hit in the head by a piece of flying debris. Cover your head and neck with a sleeping bag, blanket or anything else you have that can provide padding. Anything is better than nothing.

HOW TO SURVIVE A LIGHTNING STORM OUTDOORS

BOLT OF LIGHTNING streaking across the sky can make a striking sight, but it's also a potential danger to anyone outside. Here's how you can reduce your risk of getting struck.

1. *STAY LOW*

When lightning strikes, it's more likely to hit the taller objects in the area. Stay away from solitary trees, hilltops, radio towers or anything else that seems a likely target. A good place to take cover is in the middle of a forest, where the numerous trees will provide plenty of other places for the lightning to strike.

Lightning may look cool, but it's best observed from a safe place.

2. DITCH ANY METAL

Nothing attracts lightning like metal, so if you see a storm coming and can't find any shelter, you can decrease the chance of getting hit by dropping any metal objects you're carrying (pots, knives, jewelry, umbrellas, etc.) and putting distance between yourself and your belongings. You can always go back to collect them after danger has passed.

3. KEEP YOUR DISTANCE

Our bodies can conduct electricity easily, and if you're too close to someone who is hit by lightning, it can jump to you and give a dangerous shock! If you're with a group of people, spread out at least 50 feet from each other.

4. CROUCH DOWN

Once you've reached the best shelter you can find, further protect yourself by minimizing the surface area of your body. Crouch down on the balls of your feet and cover your ears with your hands to protect your hearing from the thunder that accompanies a nearby lightning strike.

HOW TO SAVE SOMEONE FROM DROWNING

HE WATER PROVIDES a lot of fun and good times, but it can be dangerous to even experienced swimmers. Here's how to help someone in trouble while protecting yourself!

1. *DON'T GET TOO CLOSE*
You might think saving someone from drowning involves you jumping straight into the water, swimming up to the victim, grabbing them and pulling them to safety. But drowning people aren't thinking clearly, and will often grab their would-be rescuers and hold on for dear life, putting you both in danger.

2. REACH OUT (BUT NOT WITH YOUR HAND)
The safest way to help someone drowning is to find an object they can hold on to and extend it to them. Ideally the victim is close enough so you can do this without having to get in the water. If not, grab a towel or shirt and swim out to the victim. Without getting too close, throw them one end of whatever object you've brought with you, then tow the person back to shore.

3. CHECK FOR VITALS
If the person lost consciousness before you made it to land, check their vitals as soon as you're out of the water. Roll the victim on their back and put your index and middle finger on their neck about halfway between their ear and jaw. You should  hopefully feel a pulse, but if not, find an adult immediately and tell them the victim needs CPR. In either case, call 911.

HOW TO ESCAPE A

 EXT TIME YOU take a dip in the ocean, don't let a sneaky riptide take you out to sea. A riptide is a strong current of water that cuts through the waves and pulls away from shore.

1. *DON'T FIGHT IT*
Although your first instinct may be to swim against the riptide back to shore, you're just going to tire yourself out. These tides pull at an average of 8 feet per second, so not even the strongest swimmer can overcome their might. Stay calm and get ready to sneak away from the riptide.

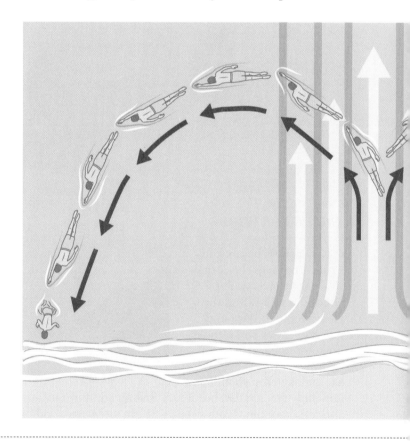

RIPTIDE

2. SIDEWAYS IS RIGHTWAYS

Instead of swimming against the riptide by heading back to the shoreline, swim parallel to the shore (either to your left or right). The tide will pull you farther out to sea while you swim sideways, but that's OK—you'll soon swim clear of the current and will be able to make your way back to shore.

3. BACK TO THE BEACH

Once you no longer feel the current pulling at you, head back to land. For extra safety, swim diagonally toward the beach so you don't risk falling in the clutches of the riptide again.

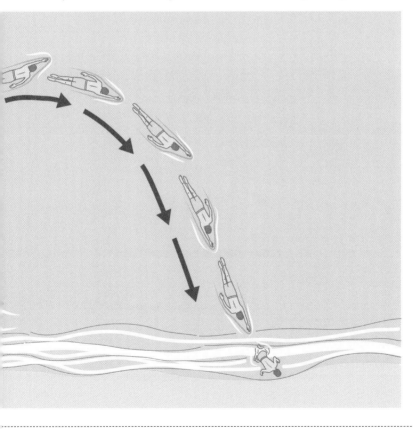

HOW TO FISH

 HETHER YOU'RE throwing them back in the water or putting them on your dinner plate, fish provide an endless source of entertainment when you're outdoors!

1. *FIND YOUR SPOT*
The first order of business with fishing is finding where they live! That's in the water, naturally, so you'll want to explore any public ponds, lakes or rivers for good fishing spots. Look for someplace without a lot of human activity or commotion to disturb the fish. It's also helpful to time your fishing expedition so it happens either at dawn or at sunset, when fish tend to be the most active.

2. BRING YOUR GEAR

While some people catch fish with their bare hands, you'll probably want to use a rod. There are lots of different types, but in the end you just need something to which you attach your hook and bait. You can use live bait—worms, crickets or other critters—but if that sounds too messy, there are artificial lures you can use as well. Just make sure you bring something to attract the fish, otherwise you'll just be sitting by a lake all day.

3. CAST YOUR LINE

Grasp the rod in your dominant hand and use your index finger to hold the line to the rod. Then with your index finger still holding the line, swing the rod back past your shoulder and sweep it forward, releasing your index finger as you extend your arm. You've cast your first line!

4. BE PATIENT

Now you need to wait for the fish to take your bait. If you feel a big tug on your rod, that could be a fish biting! Jerk the fishing pole up so there's tension in the line and start reeling the fish in. Good luck!

HOW TO MAKE A FISHING SPEAR

HERE'S MORE THAN one way to catch a fish. If you want to get up close and personal, there's no better way than using a spear. Plus, Mother Nature has the materials you'll need.

1. CHOOSE THE RIGHT WOOD

If you want the best fishing spear you can make, choose a long, thin, straight piece of wood—think of something that resembles the handle of a mop or broom. If there's a sapling (a baby tree), they usually work best because live wood is less brittle than deadwood and won't snap easily.

2. MAKE YOUR CUTS

Rest the wood on a surface and steady it with your non-dominant hand. Using your knife, make a vertical cut at one end of the wood. Keep your steadying hand far from the blade. Gently keep cutting down until you create a split about 6 inches long. Be careful that you don't split the entire piece of wood. Once you've finished that initial cut, make a horizontal cut at the same end of the wood. Again, gently cut downward for about 6 inches.

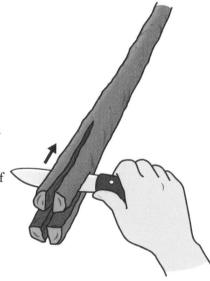

3. *GIVE A WEDGIE*
Your next order of business is to spread out the prongs of your spear. Find two twigs or small branches. Take one and wedge it down into the center of the spear as much as you can. Then take the second twig and do the same, only it should lie perpendicular to the first twig so they form a cross.

4. *STAY SHARP*
Take your knife and start sharpening each end of your spear's prongs. Remember to stay safe and always cut away from yourself!

SPEARING TIP
Water distorts images, so you'll need to aim the tip of your spear just below where the fish appears to be. Spear the broadest part of the fish.

HOW TO HANDLE BEING LOST

HE NEXT TIME you get turned around when you're out in the wild, don't panic. Your surroundings can show you the way back. Just follow these tips to get yourself back on track.

1. *STAY CALM*

First things first—you need to keep a level head on your shoulders. Running around in a blind panic won't get you out of the pickle you're in and will probably make the situation worse. No matter how lost you feel, you can always get your bearings, even if it takes longer than you'd like.

Study photos of the area you plan to explore before heading out.

YOU ARE HERE

Look around you and see if you can recognize any landmarks, whether that's a lake, a river, a mountain or even signs like the ones below.

2. STAY PUT (IF YOU CAN)
Always tell at least one adult where you intend to hike, what time you're leaving and what time you'll be back. If you get lost and stay put, you'll likely be found within a day. Never hike alone. Always bring a whistle, a map, snacks and water whenever you head out. Wandering around in the wilderness creates more risk than it's worth. Make yourself as comfortable as you can—sit or lie down to save your energy. However, if nobody knows where you are, you might need to signal for help (see pg. 84).

3. LISTEN, THEN GET LOUD
Can you hear anyone calling for you? Blow your whistle (see pg. 84), holler and be as detailed as you can as you describe your surroundings. Trying to find your rescuers by following their voices might lead you farther away, so let the help come to you.

Fresh footprints can help lead you back.

LOCATED LAKE –10 MI.

SAFE CITY – 16 MI.

RESCUED ROAD – 12 MI.

SURVIVORVILLE – 24 MI.

HOW TO HAVE A SAFE CAMPING TRIP

HE GREAT OUTDOORS can provide anything you need for a hoot and a holler—from fishing to hiking and more. Here's how you can enjoy yourself and stay safe.

1. *MAKE SURE TO DRINK WATER*
Running around outdoors can make you work up a sweat, and you want to make sure you stay hydrated by taking plenty of water with you. You should drink around 1.5 liters a day, or around two big bottles. Don't gulp it down all at once though! Just take a swig or two whenever you feel thirsty or stop for a rest.

2. *DON'T WANDER OFF TOO FAR*
Getting lost in the wilderness is nobody's idea of a good time. While you should have fun exploring nature, don't wander too far from an adult. Have a way to keep in touch: Walkie-talkies can be a good way for you to stay in communication with your adult without having to actually hang around them.

John Wayne and a group of students gather around the campfire during his visit to Meath School in Ottershaw, England, October 28, 1960.

3. LOOK, BUT DON'T TOUCH

There are a lot of beautiful plants and flowers out in the wilderness, but you'll want to ask an adult before grabbing everything in sight. They can help identify if the plant is safe to touch (pg. 46). Otherwise, you might end up with a handful of poison ivy and spend the rest of your trip scratching yourself!

When it comes to critters and bigger animals, you should always keep your distance and never try to pet or feed anything, even if it doesn't look dangerous. Even something as harmless-looking as a wild deer can carry ticks and other disease-bearing parasites you'll want to stay clear of.

4. CLEAN UP AFTER YOURSELF

Speaking of animals and food, make sure you don't leave any food scraps or leftovers lying around the campsite before you go to bed. Otherwise, your wake-up call might be the hungry growl of a bear or some other big beast. Any trash or food should be stored in sealable bags and then suspended to keep hungry creatures from getting into it (pg. 32). That way, you leave Mother Nature just as you found her for others to enjoy.

HOW TO SIGNAL FOR HELP

 ART OF BEING an expert in the outdoors is knowing when to ask for help, especially when you're lost. Here are some different ways to get attention when you need it most.

1. *BLOW THE WHISTLE*

Before heading out on your trip, one of the items you should make sure to bring with you is a whistle. It's easy to carry and, if you're lost in the wilderness, it can possibly save your life. The accepted SOS signal is to blow three times, for three seconds each, until someone can hone in on your location.

2. *SHINE A LIGHT*

Another easy-to-carry object you should always take with you is a signal mirror. To use this properly, take the mirror, place it next to your eye, then face the sun. Next, stretch out the hand that's not holding the mirror and look at it (with the mirror still held against your face). Move it around until you see the light reflected on your hand. Now make a "V" with the index and middle fingers of your outstretched hand. You'll use this to help aim the light. Place the person you want to signal to in between the "V," then aim the reflected light so it also shines between the "V." Then shift the mirror up and down three times to flash the light for an SOS signal.

3. *MAKE A SMOKY FIRE*

If you have the time and means to make a fire (see pg. 22), this makes for a great way to send a smoky signal to any would-be rescuers. Just remember that you want your fire to produce as much smoke as possible, so the dry and dead wood you'd normally want to use isn't as helpful here. Try to burn leafy, green wood and any dry sticks and leaves you can find to generate a bunch of smoke.

Seek help right away—you'll be much harder to find at night.

HOW TO IDENTIFY

EARN HOW to tell if a storm's coming with just a glance at the sky.

GOOD SIGNS
While nothing in life is certain, spotting the following cloud types in the sky means there's a good chance the weather will stay clear in the near term.

Cumulus
These clouds look like big fluffy balls of cotton and will hang low in the sky.

BAD NEWS
If you spot any of these clouds, start thinking about where to shelter for the incoming storm.

Altostratus
If the sky looks like it is covered in one big gray blanket, then there's a decent chance a rainstorm is on its way.

DANGEROUS CLOUDS

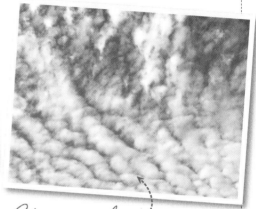

Altocumulus

If you see what looks like row after row of fluffy clouds high in the sky, you're seeing altocumulus clouds.

Cirrocumulus

These clouds usually appear when it's cold out, and look almost like thin sheets hung very high in the sky.

Nimbostratus

Similar to altostratus, except these clouds are darker and hang lower to the ground.

Cumulonimbus

While these majestic clouds look like beautiful mountains, they mean trouble for anyone caught out in the open. Cumulonimbus clouds form when warm and moist air rises high in the sky—a perfect recipe for a major storm.

HOW TO MAKE A WATER STILL

F YOU FIND yourself in an emergency situation, knowing how to make a water still can mean the difference between life and death. Here's how to quench your thirst and carry on.

1. *FIND A GOOD SPOT*

A water still is simply a hole in the ground warmed by the sun, which causes water to form that you then collect and drink. You'll want to find a patch of ground that sees plenty of sunshine and is also wet.

2. *GET DIGGING*

You'll need to dig a pit, ideally around 4 feet wide and 3 feet deep. However, you'll need to cover this pit with a plastic sheet, so if you don't have one that can stretch out to cover a hole that wide, adjust the width of the pit.

At the bottom of the pit, dig another hole where you can place a container (like an empty bottle, a cooking pot or anything that can catch water). This smaller hole should come up to about a third of the height of the container so it stays in place.

3. COVER IT UP

Cover the hole with any sort of plastic sheet you might have on you. Anchor the corners of the sheets with rocks, then place a small rock in the middle of the sheet so it forms a funnel. Just make sure the bottom of the sheet doesn't touch the dirt!

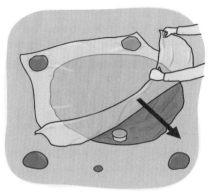

4. WAIT IT OUT

Now you need to sit back and let the sun do its thing. The heat from the sun should cause the moisture in the pit to form water, which is trapped by the plastic sheet and funneled into your container. This should create up to one liter of water a day, so it isn't much, but it could be enough to keep you alive.

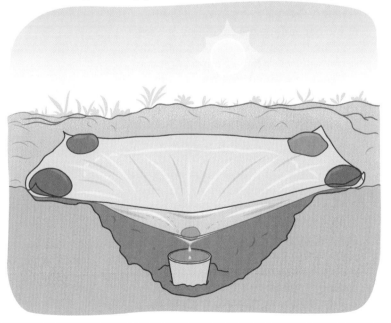

HOW TO RECOGNIZE ANIMAL TRACKS

HETHER HIKING in the woods or in your backyard, you can learn how to identify what kind of critter has been in the area by looking at the prints they've left behind. Watch out for bears!

1. *DEEPER MEANS BIGGER*

As a general rule, you can guess the size of the animal by the track it left behind. Heavier animals leave deeper paw prints in the ground, so it follows that a grizzly bear will leave a much bigger impression than a field mouse. Just remember this isn't an iron-clad rule and depends on the conditions of the ground. A cougar treading on hard, dry dirt will leave a lighter impression than a house cat would after a rainstorm, for example.

2. *POOCH OR PREDATOR?*

Dogs and other canines (such as wolves and coyotes) leave a track with an oblong bottom (where the animal's heel struck the ground) and four toe prints. Depending on the weight of the canine, you may also see a claw mark right above each toe mark. These claw marks are one of the best ways to tell the difference between someone's canine companion and a wolf—wolves have sharper claws and leave deeper marks.

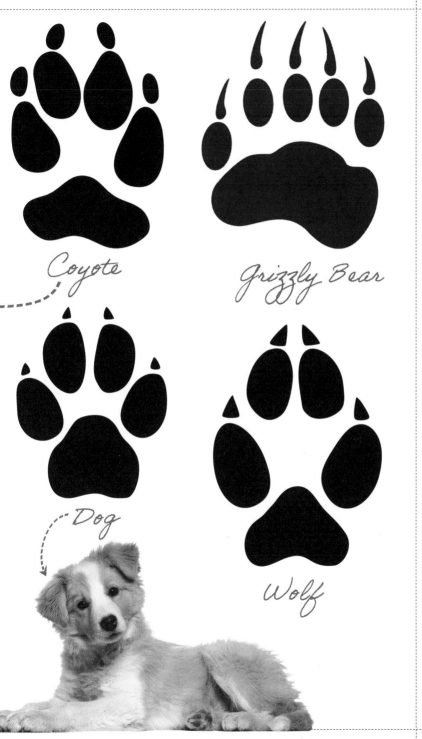

Coyote

Grizzly Bear

Dog

Wolf

3. CATS IN THE WILD

North America contains several species of wild cats, such as jaguars, cougars, ocelots and lynx. And, of course, plenty of domestic house cats prowl about the country's backyards getting into mischief. Unless your neighbor has a pet cougar, it's easy to spot the difference between tracks left by smaller domestic cats and those left by their bigger and heavier cousins in the wild. But all cat tracks can be identified by the four toes and a somewhat circular pad print.

4. HOOFING IT

Depending on where in the country you're exploring, the most plentiful tracks around will be those left by animals with hooves. Hooves are basically giant, super-sturdy nails some animals have to help protect their feet when walking. One of the most common hooved animals is the deer, and its tracks resemble two teardrop-shaped prints next to each other.

5. BEARING IT ALL

Perhaps the most important track for you to recognize in the wild of North America is that of the bear. You probably won't have much trouble spotting them in the dirt, as bears usually weigh at least a few hundred pounds. The front print of a bear track is asymmetrical with five toes, while the back paw track almost resembles a human foot—if a human foot also had five claw marks. It's pretty tough for even experienced trackers to tell the difference between a black bear and a grizzly bear, but you don't need to know the species—you just need to stay alert and be prepared to get out of there!

Horse

Ocelot

Cougar

Deer

Lynx

HOW TO READ THE TIDE

UE TO THE WAY gravity works between the moon, Earth and sun, the world's ocean levels rise and fall throughout the day. Here's how to spot whether the tide is coming in or out (and whether you should start building that sandcastle now or hold off until later).

1. USE A CHEAT SHEET

If you're able to plan ahead, the most accurate way to figure out the tide is to look up a tide table for the local beach where you're planning on playing. Scientists studying the ocean create these tables, which tell you the predicted high and low tide times for specific areas and are usually published in the newspaper. An easier way to find these tables is on the website for the National Oceanic and Atmospheric Administration: *tidesandcurrents.noaa.gov.*

2. WATCH THE RIPPLES

One way to guess the nature of the tide by just looking at the water is to observe the ripples on its surface. If the water is calm during a rising tide, you should spot small, light-colored ripples moving in the direction of the shore. These

can be tough to spot, and if there are a lot of boats or swimmers in the area, then you might need to find a spot with less activity.

3. *CLUTTER CLUES*

Take a look at the beach where the water meets the land. Do you spot a lot of seaweed, plants or other detritus (a fancy-sounding word that means "stuff") lying on the sand? That's a sign

that the tide is coming in and pushing all of that junk onto the beach. When the tide recedes, it takes a lot of that clutter back into the ocean, so a clean and tidy beach might be a sign of a falling tide.

Be wary of big waves before getting in the water.

HOW TO MAKE A BOW AND ARROW

OU'LL DEFINITELY want some adult supervision for this skill, but being able to craft this helpful hunting tool is a major achievement worth mastering.

1. *START STRONG (AND FLEXIBLE)*

For your bow, you need to strike the right balance between strength and flexibility. Your best bet is to find a sapling that's about as tall as you are and chop it down with your knife. You can test if you've got the right kind of wood by bending it and seeing if it springs back into shape quickly. If it does, you can stop your searching.

2. *FIND THE NATURAL CURVE*

Take your piece of wood and place one end on the ground while holding the wood upright with your hand. Take your free hand and push on the wood near its center until it rotates. It should stop rotating on the natural bend of the wood. The side of the wood facing you is called the "belly" of the bow, while the side facing away from you is

called the "back." Take your knife and cut one notch three inches above the center of the belly and another notch three inches below that center point.

3. CARVE UP THE BELLY

Bend the wood again and pay attention to where the wood doesn't bend on the belly or the sides. Take your knife and carefully whittle those areas away so that every part of the belly and the sides of the bow bend. The upper and lower parts of the bow should have the same thickness when you're done.

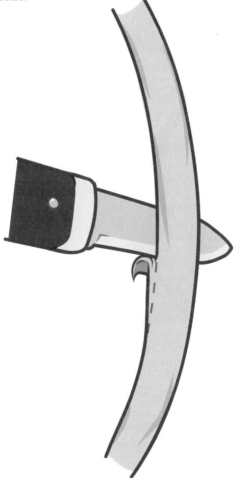

4. *MAKE A NOTCH*

At each end of the bow, cut at a 45-degree angle starting at the side of the bow and ending at the belly side. Now take your twine, shoelaces or whatever you will use as a bowstring and tie it tightly to each notch you've made. The string should be slightly shorter than the bow is long, so that it bends the bow when you pull back on it.

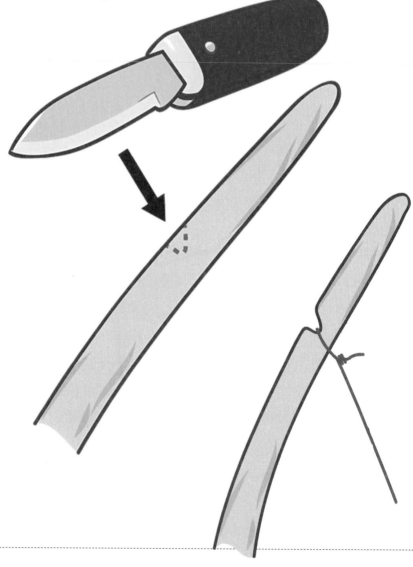

5. *GET SOME ARROWS*

In a survival situation where you need to hunt game, having arrows that fly straight can help make sure you have a full belly in the wild. Find a small branch or piece of wood you can whittle until it's as straight as possible, then sharpen one end. Make a small notch at the other end of the arrow where it will fit against your bowstring. You can also tie a bunch of pine needles right above this notch to help the arrow fly straight.

HOW TO TIE KNOTS

NOWING HOW to tie the right knot in any situation will be a huge help when navigating the outdoors! Here are a few of the most common—and useful—knots you should know.

1. *CLOVE HITCH*

You can use this knot to secure a line on a post or small tree trunk.

1. Pass the end of the rope around the post
2. Bring the rope around and cross it over itself
3. Bring the rope behind and to the left of the other end
4. Tuck it under to form a half hitch
5. Pull the ends to tighten the knot

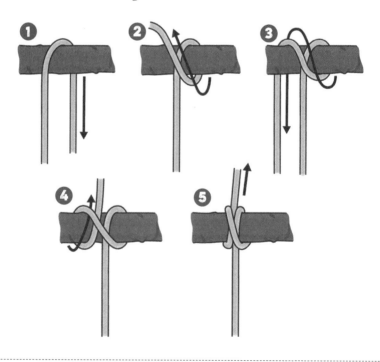

2. *TAUT LINE HITCH*

This knot is helpful for securing the stakes of your tent when camping.

1. Pass the end of the rope around the stake
2. A foot or so away from the stake, bring the rope under and then over itself once
3. Bring the free end of the rope under and over again
4. Take the free end of the rope and bring it under and over just outside of the coils you've created in the steps above
5. Tighten the knot

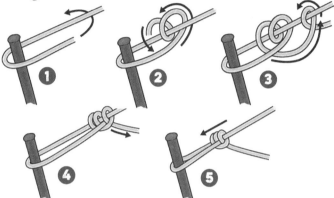

3. *TIMBER HITCH*

Turn to this knot when you need help dragging large pieces of wood.

1. Place the rope behind the wood
2. Pass the bottom end of the rope over the wood, under the top end of the rope and then over the top end
3. Tuck the same end under itself against the wood
4. Wrap the end around the cross point two more times
5. Pull ends to tighten

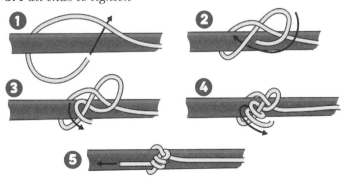

HOW TO PROTECT YOURSELF FROM THE SUN

 OTHING HURTS WORSE than scorched skin from a sunburn, and prolonged exposure to the sun over time can have a negative impact on your overall health. Be sure to follow these tips on how to block the blaze.

1. *LOVE THE LOTION*

The best way to prevent sunburn while outside is to make sure you apply plenty of sunscreen. Any part of your body that's directly exposed to sunlight should get a good slather of sunscreen rated SPF 30 or higher. Remember to apply it to your face, ears, feet (if they aren't covered by shoes) and the back of your neck. You should do this 15 to 30 minutes before heading into the sun. Remember to reapply about every two hours.

2. *DRESS UP*

Another best practice for avoiding sunburn is to cover up as much of your body as you can. You want to make sure you don't overdo it—hiking in a heavy hoodie on a summer day won't be any fun. But if you can wear a hat, long sleeves, sunglasses and shoes (not flip-flops), those will go a long way toward cutting down your exposure to the sun's rays.

3. *TAKE A SIESTA*

If the sun's beating down something fierce, sometimes the best thing to do is simply stay in the shade! Chilling out for a few hours before and after noon means you get plenty of rest and are more likely to stay sunburn-free.

1. Wear sunscreen

Always be sure to wear SPF 30 or higher when outside. It's important to apply it 30 minutes before heading out, and be sure to reapply it every two hours or directly after swimming or sweating excessively.

2. Wear a hat

Wearing a hat protects your scalp, and a hat with a wide brim provides protection for your face, neck, ears and shoulders.

3. Wear sunglasses

Our eyes are susceptible to sun damage and skin cancer on the eyelids, so we want to be sure we wear sunglasses when outside, especially around water or snow as those surfaces reflect UV rays.

4. Cover with clothing

Wearing long sleeves and long pants is a great way to cover most of your body when outdoors. If you are swimming or surfing, wear a rashguard or a wet suit as it is meant to be worn in the water, which will cover a majority of the otherwise exposed skin.

5. Seek shade

Try to sit under an umbrella or tree when you are outside. Remember, clouds are not a good source of shade, as 80 percent of UV rays can penetrate clouds. So although clouds may block the brightness and heat of the sun, they do not provide adequate shade protection.

John Wayne on the set of *Hondo* (1953).

John Wayne on the set of his classic 1953 film *Hondo*.

SELF-SUFFICIENCY AT HOME

TAKE CARE OF THINGS ON THE HOME FRONT BY MASTERING THESE TIMELESS TIPS

HOW TO HAMMER A NAIL

F ALL YOU have is a hammer, then every problem looks like a nail. But sometimes your problem is a nail. Here's how to handle it.

1. *HOLD IT RIGHT*

Keep a firm grip on the hammer. If you want more control (when you're getting the nail started, for example) hold the hammer closer to its head. The farther away from the head you hold the handle, the harder you'll drive the nail.

> **LET THE HAMMER DO THE WORK!**
> Allow the weight and momentum of the hammer to do a lot of the work and you'll be able to work twice as hard with half the effort.

> Never rush or try to multitask while using a hammer.

2. *TAP TAP*

Using your non-dominant hand, hold the nail gently between your thumb and forefinger. Place the nail on the spot where you want to drive it down, then lightly tap the head of the nail with the hammer until the nail digs into the surface just enough to keep it upright without you having to hold it.

3. *GO TO TOWN*

Swing the hammer from your elbow to bring down more force on the nail, but make sure you don't swing so hard that you miss the nail! Keep going until the nail is flush with the surface, then call it quits, otherwise you risk leaving hammer-sized dents in the surface.

HOW TO USE A HAND SAW

K **NOW HOW TO** cut wood down to just the right size with the help of a trusty hand saw.

ASK AN ADULT FOR HELP, PILGRIM!

1. MAKE YOUR MARK

If you're using a hand saw for a craft project, such as building a birdhouse, then you'll need to be exact in how much wood you're cutting with the saw. Make sure to use a ruler or measuring tape to gauge how much wood you need to saw off, and then use a pencil to draw a line marking the full length of the cut (measure twice, cut once as the saying goes). You don't want to eyeball things and end up ruining the piece of wood.

Make sure your support hand is a good distance from the blade.

2. CLAMP IT DOWN

Place the piece of wood on a flat surface (such as a workbench or an old table) and secure the wood so it doesn't wiggle from the force of your sawing. Clamps from your local hardware store work best, but in a pinch, you can try placing a heavy object on the part of the wood farthest from where you will be sawing.

3. HOLD ON AND LINE UP

Grab the saw by its handle using your dominant hand and stand over the piece of wood. Place your other hand on the wood to give it some extra stability for when you start sawing. Make sure this hand is well clear of the saw blade or you could get badly hurt! Your shoulder, arm and hand should form a line with the saw blade, which should be at a 45-degree angle to the wood.

4. GET TO WORK

Place the saw blade along the measurement line you drew earlier and give it a few short pulls backward. After a few of these back cuts, there should be a notch in the wood. Now you can begin sawing using a smooth back-and-forth motion, drawing your elbow toward you, then pushing the saw toward the wood. The longer your stroke, the faster you'll cut. Don't try to force things—you want the momentum of the saw to do most of the work for you.

PICK A SIDE!

The saw you're using is probably thin, but if you don't slice along the side of the measurement line you've drawn, your cuts will be off by the width of the saw blade! That's why it's always best to align your blade on the right side (or left, if you're left-handed) side of the measurement line.

HOW TO PUT OUT A GREASE FIRE

HESE BLAZES CAN get out of control very quickly. When you're cooking on the stove, be prepared for the possibility of major flames so you can save your bacon.

1. SMOTHER IT SAFELY

If the fire seems small (think contained to one pan vs. flames covering the entire stove top), try to quickly cover the flames with a metal lid. You don't have to use the lid that matches with the pot or pan—a cookie tray or baking sheet will work just as well. Whatever you can get to fast. The goal is to cover the flames and starve the fire of oxygen.

Try not to let your cooking oil get too hot in the first place.

2. SALT AND SODA

If you're able to trap the fire under a metal container, you can deliver a knockout blow by dumping baking soda or salt on the flames. Just make dead certain you're throwing baking soda into the fire and not flour, otherwise you'll be feeding the inferno instead of extinguishing it.

3. GET OUT

While you can possibly contain a small grease fire, the situation can easily spiral out of control. If at any point you feel like you can't put out the fire, don't hesitate to leave your house or apartment immediately. Call 911 using a cell phone or a neighbor's phone, and let the professionals do their job.

SAY NO TO H_2O

Never use water to put out a grease fire. Water and oil don't mix, meaning you can't directly lower the temperature of the fire's fuel using H_2O. In fact, tossing water onto a grease fire will likely spread it, putting you in greater danger.

Baking Soda

HOW TO MAKE BACON AND EGGS

 EARN TO MAKE a simple and satisfying breakfast and you may never look at cereal the same way.

ASK AN ADULT FOR HELP, PILGRIM!

1. *BACON THEN EGGS*

Frying up your bacon first lets you cook the eggs in delicious bacon grease, so start with the meat. Take the bacon out of the refrigerator and let it sit on the countertop for about 15 minutes until it's close to room temperature. Peel off a few slices of bacon and place them in a non-stick frying pan. Now wash your hands with soap and warm water (you've just touched raw meat) and get ready to cook.

2. HEAT THINGS UP
Make sure the bacon's arranged in the pan so the slices aren't touching each other (it's fine if they do a little, but you want to give them as much room as possible). Turn the heat to medium and wait for the bacon to  start sizzling. Once it does, turn the heat down to low—if bacon grease starts splattering loudly and flying about, you'll know you have the heat on too high, and it could lead to a grease fire (pg. 110). Using a pair of tongs, flip the pieces of bacon every couple of minutes until they're as crispy as you like. Depending on how thick the slices are, this should take 10 to 15 minutes.

3. FRYING WITH FAT
Use tongs to place the cooked bacon on a plate. Then take two or three eggs, crack them (one at a time) on the kitchen countertop and empty the eggs into the frying pan full of bacon fat. Use a spoon to cover the eggs in fat and wait for the eggs to cook. It should take about three minutes before the whites of the eggs firm up and the edges start to curl—a telltale sign that the eggs are ready to eat. Use a spatula to transfer the eggs from the pan to the plate and enjoy!

HOW TO COOK EGGS

Eggs cook quickly, so be sure to keep an eye on them in the pan. Leave them alone until the whites set up, about 3 minutes. For sunny-side-up eggs, take them out of the pan after the 3 minutes is up; for over-easy, flip them at the 3-minute mark, then cook for another 30 seconds; for over-medium, flip them at the 3-minute mark and cook for 1 minute; and for over-hard, flip them at the 3-minute mark, then cook for 2 to 3 minutes. If you make a mistake, that's OK—you can always scramble them and they'll still taste great.

HOW TO IRON A T-SHIRT AND PANTS

EEP YOURSELF looking sharp by learning how to ditch those pesky wrinkles. Not only will you look nice, you'll also please your parents by giving them one less thing to do!

1. *ALL ABOARD!*

While any flat surface can do in a pinch, an ironing board is the best place to lay your T-shirt for ironing. You want the end of the ironing board to enter the shirt through the hole at its bottom, almost like the ironing board was wearing the shirt. Smooth out any wrinkles on the shirt by hand and make sure your iron is set to the temperature that's right for the shirt's material (you can check your shirt for a tag in case you aren't sure what it's made of).

2. *HOLD STILL*

Take the hot iron and start ironing. Unlike when ironing a dress shirt, you don't want to move the iron over the shirt. Instead, press the iron to a section of a shirt for a few seconds, then lift it up and move on to the next section of the shirt. Shift the shirt around the ironing board until you've pressed the entire tee. Then take it off the board and place it somewhere flat (like your bed) to let it cool.

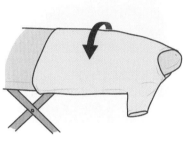

3. *FANCY PANTS*

Take the pair of pants you want ironed and lay them flat lengthwise on the ironing board. Press the iron for a few seconds on the area near the waistband to get rid of any wrinkles there. Then take the iron and slowly move down one of the pant legs, making sure the pant leg stays flat against the board. Do the same with the other leg, then flip the pants and repeat the process. Done!

HOW TO SEW A BUTTON

ON'T LET A MISSING button stop you from looking buttoned up. With a few simple materials and the help of these easy steps, you can become a sewing pro in no time.

1. GET YOUR SUPPLIES

Gather together a sewing needle, thread, a pair of scissors (or pocket knife) and a button. Unspool some thread, about the length of your forearm, then snip it.

2. THREAD IT

Pull the thread through the eye of the needle until the two ends are aligned. Then tie the two ends together so you have a knot at the opposite end of the needle.

3. BUTTON IT UP

Take the button and place it on top of the area where the original button fell off. Hold the needle's point against the underside of the cloth and push it through one of the button's holes. Pull the thread through, stopping when the knotted end is against the cloth.

4. FILL THOSE HOLES

Now take the needle and put it through the hole diagonal to the one you already pulled it through. Remember to pull the entire needle and thread

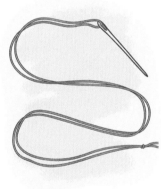

through the hole to keep the thread pulled tight. Repeat this for the two remaining holes, pushing up through the cloth and hole and then putting the point through the other hole so the thread is wrapped tightly against the button. You can repeat this process a few more times, alternating sides, until the button feels secure.

5. *ONE LAST PUSH*
When you're done with the last pass and the needle is on the underside of the fabric, carefully slide it between the sewn thread and the fabric. Pull tight and repeat but leave a little bit of room. Now insert the needle through the loop you've created and pull tight to tie off a knot. Cut the thread above the knot and you're done!

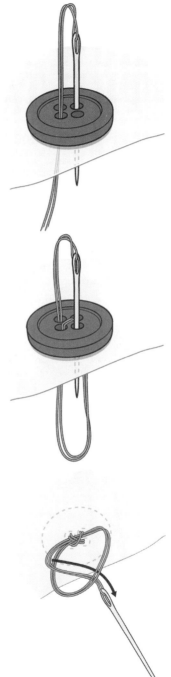

HOW TO SET THE TABLE

EXT TIME YOU'RE asked to get the table ready for dinner, show off your knowledge by following these tips.

1. *PLACE MATS FIRST*

Avoid scratching up the dining room table with silverware by putting down a place mat for each person before moving on to the next steps. If there's a tablecloth on the table you can consider skipping this step.

2. PLATES AND NAPKINS

Put one plate in the middle of each place mat so you're leaving plenty of room for the silverware and napkins. Place one folded napkin to the left of each plate. You should fold the napkin in half diagonally so it looks like a triangle (if using cloth as opposed to paper napkins, fold your triangle in half again). The longest side should face the plate. Put the salad plate on top of the dinner plate.

3. FORKS, KNIVES AND SPOONS

Place the fork on top of the napkin. If you're using salad forks (which are smaller than dinner forks), place the salad fork to the left of the dinner fork. On the right side of the plate, place the knife with the blade facing toward the plate. To the right of the knife, place the spoon.

4. BREAD PLATE

If you're using a bread plate and knife, put the bread plate above the fork and napkin, with the bread knife lying across the center of the bread plate with its blade facing toward the napkins and forks.

5. GLASSWARE

Now place the water glass above the dinner plate and knife on the right side of the plate, so that it's lined up between the plate and knife. The juice glass can go to the left of the water glass.

HOW TO CLEAN YOUR BATHROOM

J **UST BECAUSE THE** bathroom is where you do your dirty work doesn't mean it has to be filthy. Read on to discover how you can keep everything sparkling clean.

1. *EMPTY IT OUT*
First things first: Remove any towels, toothbrushes, combs, rugs, etc. from the bathroom so that there's nothing between you and the surfaces you need to clean. Put everything in a pile in another room and get to work, first ensuring the bathroom is well-ventilated (you can also open a window) as you don't want to inhale too much of the cleaners you'll be using.

2. *SOAK IT*
Get a bottle of all-purpose bathroom cleaner and start spraying the shower and inside of the toilet bowl. Next, take a rag, spray it with the cleaner until it's damp and wipe down the sink and any other surfaces (but not the toilet bowl yet!).

3. *NICE AND SHINY*
For the mirrors, you'll need a bottle of streak-free glass cleaner and another rag. Spray the cleaner directly on the surface of the mirror, and then wipe it down with a rag. Work in

sections, so that you're spraying and wiping constantly, which will help prevent the spray from running down the mirror and leaving streaks.

4. DOWN WITH DIRT
Head back to the shower, where the stuff you want to clean (mildew, soap scum, probably some hair) has been softened from the cleaner you sprayed it with a few minutes ago. Take your rag and put some elbow grease in cleaning things up, then use a toilet brush and scrub the inside bowl of the toilet. Don't forget to clean under the toilet bowl's edges—you might be amazed (aka completely grossed out) by what you knock loose!

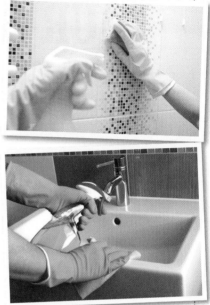

5. EXIT STRATEGY
Now get down on your hands and knees and start wiping down the floor with a rag soaked in cleaning solution. You should begin this at the corner of the bathroom farthest from the door and work your way toward the exit.

6. LAST LOOKS
With a new rag and some hot water, wipe down any of the items you removed from the bathroom before you started cleaning so you can get the bits of toothpaste and other bathroom grime off them.

HOW TO FOLD YOUR CLOTHES

HERE'S NO SENSE doing your laundry if you're just going to toss clean clothes into a messy pile. Here's how to make sure the stuff you store stays looking sharp.

1. *THE T-SHIRT*
Lay the shirt face down and fold the right half of it to the center. Turn the sleeve so it faces toward the outside edge of the shirt. Repeat this with the right side. Take the bottom half and fold it up to where the two sleeves meet. Then fold the top half over that so the neck is visible.

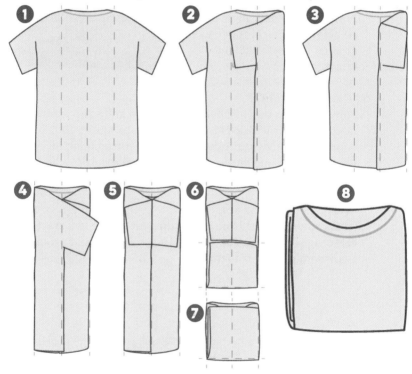

2. *PANTS AND SHORTS*

Place the pants or shorts on a flat surface. Start at either the left or right end and fold them across horizontally, so that the seams all match up. Then fold up vertically from the bottom of the leg once, and then up from the bottom once again.

FOLD WHILE WARM

Clothes that are fresh out of the dryer are at their softest and most wrinkle-free. Leave them out and you risk needing to iron out unsightly creases.

HOW TO SHINE YOUR SHOES

Y **OU LIKELY WON'T** wear dress shoes all the time. When you do, it will be for a special occasion, such as a school dance or a relative's wedding. Here's how to make the moment count.

1. *GATHER YOUR TOOLS*
Get a shoe brush, a soft rag (or old T-shirt), leather cleaner and conditioner, shoe polish and wax. It's a pretty hefty list of items to buy, but many stores sell a shoeshine kit to simplify the process.

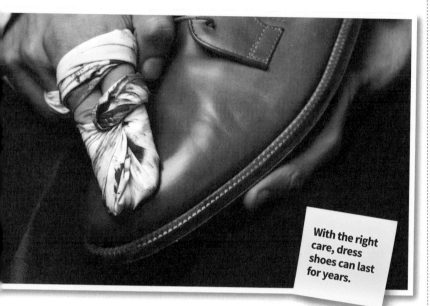

With the right care, dress shoes can last for years.

2. KEEP THINGS CLEAN

Shoe polish does a great job of adding color to your kicks, but it also is fantastic for staining the carpet and furniture, so be mindful! Cover your work area with old newspaper to prevent leaving stains that'll be tough to remove.

3. POLISH 'EM PRETTY

Remove the laces from your shoes and clean the dirt from the shoes with your brush, using leather cleaner if necessary. Take your leather conditioner and apply a thin layer to the surface of the shoe and let it sit for 10 to 20 minutes, then dab some shoe polish on a soft cloth. Apply the polish using circular motions over the entire shoe's surface. Start with the least amount of polish you think the shoe needs—you can always add more later. Use a cream polish for a softer, more subtle look. Or go for the wax if you really want to stand out in a crowd.

4. BUFF IT UP

After you've applied the polish, take the soft cloth and rub it back and forth across the surface of the shoe, removing any excess polish. Enjoy your shiny shoes!

HOW TO TIE A NECKTIE

ONE OF THOSE tricks that separates the men from the boys, tying a tie is much easier than it looks. Here's how to pull it off (well, tie it on).

WRAP AROUND
Grab your tie, face a mirror and turn up your shirt collar. Place the tie around the back of your neck with the front of the tie facing outward. The wide end of the tie should be on your right side and the skinny end on your left side. Make sure the skinny end of the tie lands just above your belly button (**1**).

❶

KEEP IT CLEAN
If you're wearing a tie at dinner you can keep it from dropping onto your plate by unbuttoning the second shirt button from the top and sliding the tie inside your shirt. You can add a napkin, tucking it into your collar, for extra coverage.

ACROSS AND OVER

Grab the wide end and pull it across your body and over the skinny end of the tie (**2**). Take the wide end under the skinny end (**3**), back across the front (**4**) and then up through the loop you created at the start of this step (**5**).

KNOT IT UP

Pull the wide end through the loop (**6**). Keep doing this until a knot has now formed in front of your chest. Grab the skinny end and pull it down while shifting the knot up your neck to tighten (**7**).

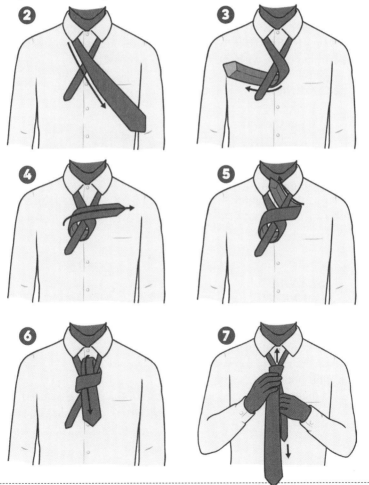

HOW TO MAKE YOUR BED

HERE ARE FEW things more rewarding in life than a good night's rest. Here's how to lay the groundwork for a shut-eye session.

1. *GET FITTED*
Place the fitted sheet (the one with the stretchy corners) over the mattress. Make sure the long side of the sheet matches up with the long side of the bed.

2. *TOP SHEET*
Take the top sheet and put the wide seam at the head of the bed. Tuck the other end of the sheet underneath the bottom of the mattress but leave the sides of the top sheet untucked.

3. *BLANKET COVERAGE*
Put your blanket on top of the top sheet and align the sides and top and bottom. Leave 6 inches of space between the top of the mattress and the top of the blankets. Tuck the bottom of the blanket in, and keep the sides untucked.

4. FOLD OVER

At the top of the bed, stretch the blanket to the inner edge of the top sheet's seam. Fold the top sheet's seam over the blanket. Make another fold at the top of the sheet, folding both the blanket and the top sheet together. You should now have a rectangular "border" between your top sheet/blanket and the bare fitted sheet.

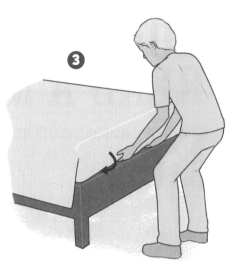

5. AND FOLD OVER AGAIN

Fold the sheet/blanket over itself one more time, which should leave about a foot and a half of space between the top of the mattress and the beginning of the top sheet. Now you can finally tuck the sides of your blanket and top sheet under the mattress.

START THE DAY RIGHT

Studies suggest that you'll be more productive throughout the day if you begin each morning by making your bed.

HOW TO READ A MAP

FINDING YOUR SENSE of direction will help keep you from getting lost, but you'll need to learn how to read a map if you want to find your way through your next adventure.

1. *HOLD THE DARN THING RIGHT*

First things first—before you can get your bearings in real life, you have to orient yourself with the map you have in your hands. Some maps feature a small image called a compass rose that tells you which side of the map is north. If your map doesn't have a compass rose, then you should assume the top of the map (when you hold the map so you can read the words written on it) is north.

Use your finger to trace potential routes you might take.

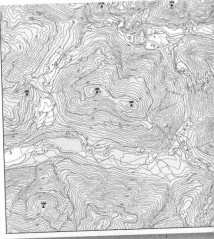

2. LEARN THE LEGEND

Next, look for a small box that lists all the different types of symbols on the map—it's usually near one of the corners. That list, called a legend, should tell you what each of those symbols mean. For example, a black line like "_____" might signify a road.

LEGEND

- Rim Rock Drive
- Trails
- Overlooks
- Distance along Rim Rock Drive
- Picnic area
- Campground
- Wheelchair access
- Ranger station

3. FIND YOURSELF

Having a map is all well and good, but it may as well be a fire starter unless you can figure out where on the map you are in real life. Take a look at what your map identifies—roads, landmarks, rivers, etc.—then take a gander at your surroundings to see if you recognize anything. If you don't, you may have to pick a direction and start walking until you come across something that lets you know where you are on the map. Just be certain you know which direction you're headed, otherwise you could end up wandering in circles and getting lost! And if you are lost, be sure to follow the guidelines detailed on pg. 84.

4. GET THE LAY OF THE LAND

Some maps might be covered in wavy, circular lines called contour lines, which tell you the elevation of the area. Contour lines separate uphill from downhill, so the inside of a contour line represents an increase in elevation, while the outside of a contour line represents a decrease. The innermost circle represents the highest point of land, and as you move outside of each circle, the elevation decreases. One more thing: The closer together the lines are, the steeper the climb (because the elevation is changing quickly). Be mindful of elevation changes once you start moving—the last thing you want to do is mistake a strenuous uphill hike for an easy stroll.

HOW TO CARE FOR A POCKET KNIFE

HERE'S MORE TO maintaining your trusty pocket knife than keeping it sharp. Find out what else you need to do to ensure your knife is ready whenever you may need it.

1. *KEEP IT CLEAN*

ASK AN ADULT FOR HELP, PILGRIM!

Depending on what you use the knife for, there's a good chance gunk and debris can build up on the blade. You can give the knife a good cleaning with nothing more than some warm water, dish soap and an old toothbrush. Mix the soap and the water, then dip the toothbrush into the mixture. Scrub the entire knife (including the handle) to get out all of the dirt. Dry it off with a thick towel so the water doesn't sit and possibly rust the knife.

Out in the wild? A body of water can provide a quick rinse.

2. *OIL BEATS RUST*

Speaking of rust, the best thing you can do to prevent it is by making sure your blade is oiled. Put some knife oil on a rag or old T-shirt, and then carefully wipe the rag along the length of the blade. Use a different rag (or the dry part of the same rag) to wipe off any excess.

Always point the blade away from you while cleaning.

HOW TO HANDLE YOUR MONEY

THAT MAKES THE WORLD go round, so you better start figuring out how it works. Knowing how to manage your cash can set you up for a lifetime of riches.

1. *HARD TO GET, EASY TO LOSE*

First things first, partner—you have to understand that for most folks, money isn't easy to come by. That's part of what makes it valuable and lets us buy things with it! The most common way for adults to earn money is through a job, but until you're old enough to work, you might get an allowance from your parents or a gift from a grandparent. Choosing what you do with what you earn is part of the fun.

2. *COME UP WITH A PLAN*

It's a big wide world out there with plenty of people willing to help you part with your money. If you don't have a plan, you could end up spending your hard-won cash on things you don't really want or need. Take a second and write down a list of everything you need to buy in a week and how much each item costs. It's important to recognize the difference between

A piggy bank will help you save your extra money.

Walter Brennan, Vera Ralston and John Wayne in *Dakota* (1945).

wants and needs: You *need* to eat lunch every day at school, whereas you *want* a new video game.

Once you have a list of everything you need to buy in a week, add all the prices together, then subtract that number from the amount of money you have. If you're lucky enough to have any money left over, then congratulations! You can spend that money on things you want (but don't need) like toys, books, candy, etc. But you might not want to rush off for a shopping spree just yet.

3. *YOU GOTTA SAVE BIG TO SPEND BIG*

After covering your basic necessities, you might be tempted to spend the rest of your cash on whatever you want—but hold your horses! Saving some of that leftover money is the key to buying some big-ticket items in the future. Each time you have a little extra money, set some aside for a future goal. The amount of money you save is up to you, but even a little bit helps! Future you will thank you.

HOW TO GIVE FIRST-RATE FIRST AID

EARN HOW TO treat almost any kind of minor scrape, injury or bite before heading to the doc.

1. *SPLINTERS*

Wash and gently dry the area. Take a close look at the splinter, using a magnifying glass if necessary, to see how it entered your skin. Take a pair of tweezers and sterilize the tips with rubbing alcohol. Using your tweezers, grab hold of the end of the splinter and gently pull it out in the same direction it entered from. Next, clean your wound with soap and water, and apply petroleum jelly.

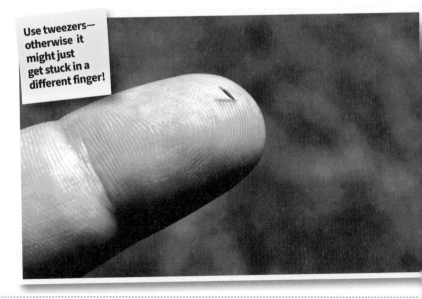

Use tweezers— otherwise it might just get stuck in a different finger!

2. BITES AND STINGS

Here's the rundown of common bites and stings and how to treat them. If you start feeling a tightness in your chest or throat, break out in a rash or otherwise start feeling sick or in pain after a bite or sting, immediately tell an adult who can get you proper medical attention.

Bee Sting

This usually looks like a red bump that is painful to touch. If you can see that the stinger is still inside your skin (it will look like a black dot), remove it by either pressing and scraping the area with a credit card (or something similar). Do not attempt to pull it out with a pair of tweezers, as you would a splinter. Doing so may squeeze venom out of the venom sac and into the wound. Wash the area with soap and water, then ask an adult to give you an over-the-counter painkiller for the discomfort and place an ice pack over the area.

Spider Bite

This will look like a red, angry welt. Keep the area clean with soap and water, apply an antibiotic cream to prevent infection and don't scratch it! Bites from a brown recluse or black widow require medical attention, however.

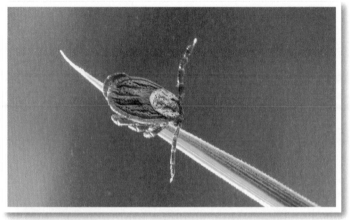

Tick Bite

This usually looks like a red bump. If the tick is attached to you, slowly remove it with a pair of tweezers in an upward motion. Place ice or a cold pack on the bite for 15 to 20 minutes every hour. If the bite starts to look like a bullseye or you get a headache or have trouble breathing, consult a doctor.

Jellyfish Sting

If you've been stung by a jellyfish, use tweezers to remove any tentacles you see on you. Then, soak the affected area of your skin in hot (but not scalding) water for 20 to 45 minutes. If the sting is on an area of the body that's difficult to keep immersed, take a shower to keep hot water on the sting for this amount of time.

3. RASHES FROM PLANTS

Plants can cause trouble for your skin either by sticking you or smearing you with something unpleasant. In the first case, spines, thorns and tiny "hairs" from plants can get under your skin and cause irritation. If you can see the spine or thorn, remove it with a pair of sterilized tweezers. If you can't, covering the area in craft glue and peeling it off after it's dried can help.

Plants such as poison sumac, ivy or oak secrete a special kind of oil that causes an itchy, painful rash. If you come into contact with these plants, immediately wash the affected area with water but not soap. Afterward, warm baths or soaking the area in warm water can help provide relief. Apply calamine lotion as needed.

KEEP AN EYE ON IT

If a rash you received from coming into contact with a poisonous plant persists, you may need to see a doctor to treat it.

HOW TO FIX A FLAT BIKE TIRE

OMETIMES WHEN THE rubber meets the road, the road wins. Here's how to repair your damaged tire and get back to riding.

1. *GIVE YOUR BIKE A BRAKE*
Start by releasing the brakes. How you do this depends on the type of brakes your bike has, but for rim brakes (the most common), you'll want to disconnect the brake calipers (the clamp-looking thing on the wheel) from the cable that runs between them. You can do this by either squeezing the calipers with your hands or by finding a quick-release lever (if your bike has one). Next, flip your bike upside-down to easily reach the parts of the wheel you'll need to work with.

2. *WHEELS OFF*
Once the brakes have been disconnected and you've turned your bike upside down, it's time to get that wheel off of the bike. If the wheel is bolted on, you'll need to find a wrench and loosen the nuts. Some bikes also have a quick-release lever on the wheel that you use to loosen things up. Once the nuts are loose, slide the wheel off the frame of the bike and place it somewhere nearby.

3. *PULL IT APART*

Now you need to create space between the tire and the wheel rim. Let the remaining air out of the tire, and then use your hands to press the edge of the tire toward the center of the rim. Keep doing this for the length of the tire, pushing it toward the center until you're able to slip the tire free from the rim far

enough for you to fit your hand inside the space created. Reach in with your hand and pull the inflatable tube apart from the tire. This tube is what you want to work with.

4. *CHECK IT OUT*

Take a look at the tube for any obvious holes or tears. If you can spot it, great! If not, fill the tube with air (using a pump or air hose) and listen—you may be able to hear where the air is escaping from. Once you've identified where the leak is, it's time to patch it up.

5. *GET ROUGH*

Take a piece of sandpaper and rub it around the area of the leak. This helps the patch you are going to place over the tear stick better. Use rubber cement (or the glue provided in a bike repair kit) and apply it over the tear. Let the glue set for a minute or two, then apply the tube patch from a bike repair kit.

6. *PUTTING IT BACK TOGETHER*

Take your good-as-new tube and place the valve stem at its end into the valve stem hole on the rim of the wheel. Then use your hands to feed the tube back under the outer tire, until it is all one tube and tire again. Reconnect the wheel and brakes and you're ready to ride!

HOW TO REMOVE A STAIN

ON'T CRY OVER spilled milk (or anything else) that's left a mess. Simply follow these steps after a spill to ensure you have things looking good as new.

1. *ACT FAST*

No matter the type of stain, you need to move quickly—a stain that dries is a stain that's much harder to remove. Start applying plenty of cold water to the stain to keep it wet while you figure out how to remove it for good. You might have to switch to warm water later depending on the type of stain, but don't worry about that now.

2. *FULL COURT PRESS*

You DO NOT want to just start scrubbing away. While there's a chance doing so can help remove the stain, all that rubbing can just as easily make things worse. Instead, blot the stain with a paper towel to try and lift the offending material from the fabric.

3. *KNOW YOUR ENEMY*

Different types of stains have different weaknesses. Here's a quick and dirty list for how to keep things looking clean:

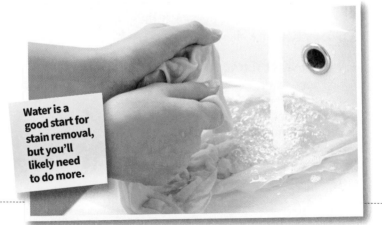

Water is a good start for stain removal, but you'll likely need to do more.

Grease

Sprinkle baking powder over the stain. Blot and lightly scrub the stain.

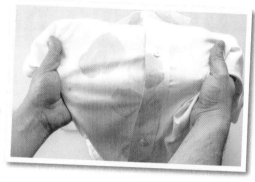

Chocolate

Mix water with some white vinegar and blot the stain.

Blood

Get some hydrogen peroxide (check the medicine cabinet), mix it with cold water, then blot the stain.

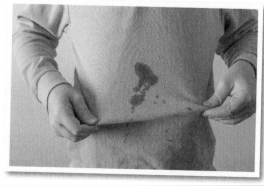

HOW TO DO A PUSH-UP, PULL-UP AND SIT-UP

MPRESS YOUR GYM teacher and build your strength by nailing these basic body weight exercises that don't require any fancy equipment or expensive memberships.

1. *THE PUSH-UP*

Get down on your hands and knees. Next, straighten your legs behind you and place your hands a little wider than shoulder width apart. Lower your body until your chest almost hits the floor. Push yourself back up using your arms. That's one.

2. THE PULL-UP

Stand below a pull-up bar. Grab the bar with the palms of your hands facing away from you (this is called an overhand grip). Your hands should be a little more than shoulder-width apart. Pull yourself up as much as you can. Lower your body. That's one.

3. THE SIT-UP

Lie flat on your back. Your legs should be out in front of you with the flats of your feet planted on the ground. Cross your arms in front of your chest. Using your abdomen muscles and keeping your feet on the ground, sit up as much as you can. That's one.

John Wayne as Capt. Dooley in the 1953 film *Island in the Sky*.

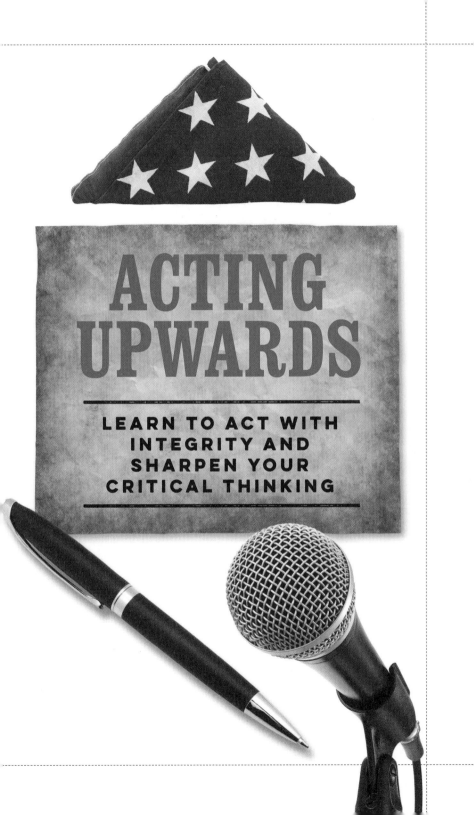

ACTING UPWARDS

LEARN TO ACT WITH INTEGRITY AND SHARPEN YOUR CRITICAL THINKING

HOW TO IMPROVE YOUR MANNERS

FEW SIMPLE tweaks to the way you carry yourself in front of others can have a lasting impact. With the help of these lessons, you can even lead others by example someday.

1. *LANGUAGE, PLEASE*

There's a reason "please" is the magic word—it's probably the one thing you can say that will almost always class up your request. You should also remember to say "thank you" when someone does you a good turn to show your gratitude.

It feels good to be polite and respectful to others.

2. IT'S NOT ABOUT YOU

The point of good manners is to show consideration and respect for people other than yourself. That means not taking the last piece of cake at the party (without asking), holding doors open for people and not interrupting when others are speaking. While it doesn't apply to every situation, the "Golden Rule"— don't do anything to others you wouldn't want them to do to you—will usually steer you toward good manners.

KEEP IT CLEAN

Don't talk or joke about anything gross in front of other people. Otherwise, you're being rude. As a general rule, if you're about to talk about something that happens in the bathroom, save it for the playground with your friends—or skip it entirely.

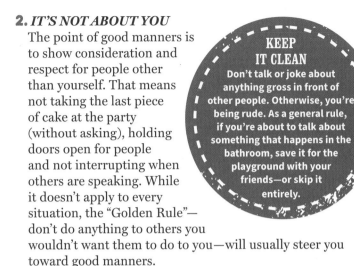

Laraine Day, John Wayne and Cedric Hardwicke in *Tycoon* (1947).

HOW TO SHOW RESPECT FOR YOUR ELDERS

HETHER THEY'RE YOUR great aunt, your grandfather or simply an older neighbor, there's a lot to gain by engaging with those who are older than you.

1. *TAKE AN INTEREST*

A simple way to show that you care is simply by paying attention. Take the time to get to know the elder by asking how their day was. When they talk, truly listen and ask follow-up questions. You probably have more in common than you think. Find shared points of interest you can enjoy together.

If you're willing to listen, you can gain a lot of wisdom from your elders.

2. *DO AS YOU'RE TOLD*
Nobody, at any age, likes being told when to take out the trash or to tidy up their room. But when you're a kid, it's part of the deal that you should do all of the chores and tasks a trusted adult asks you to complete. That doesn't mean you can't respectfully disagree with an adult's opinion, but in general, it's better to not put up a fuss and to do as you're told. The more you do, the more you'll be entrusted with bigger, more important responsibilities.

LEND A HAND

The next time you go to visit an elderly relative, ask them if there's anything you can help them with. This can include anything from performing household chores to solving a tough crossword puzzle to setting up something on their laptop or phone. Simple gestures like these are great ways to show them the respect they deserve.

3. *MIND YOUR MANNERS*
All of the rules for good manners (see pg. 148) apply when showing respect for your elders. That means chewing with your mouth closed, saying "please" and "thank you" and all of the other basics. And since many kids don't act in such a respectful manner, you'll score extra points with the elders in your life by showing some uncommon courtesy.

HOW TO THINK CRITICALLY

HE ABILITY TO REASON
through life's problems is one of our
great blessings as humans. Here's how
to ensure you don't let it go to waste.

1. *DON'T TAKE THEIR WORD FOR IT*
Thinking critically means uncovering and understanding
the logic behind why things are the way they are, not
accepting "just because" as an answer. Asking "why" and
not taking things at face value is your most powerful
tool and one you'll need to use often in order to master
critical thinking. If someone isn't able to answer you
directly, ask if they're able to help you look it up.

2. *NOT ALL ARGUMENTS*
ARE EQUAL
One trap people often fall into
when trying to think critically
is to start assuming every
argument has value, or that
there are "two sides" to every
story. Facts are facts, and
opinions are opinions—that's
why we have different words
for each.

Fact:
a thing that is known or
proved to be true.
(ex: George Washington
was the first president of
the United States.)

Opinion:
a view or judgment
formed about something,
not necessarily based on
facts or knowledge. (ex:
George Washington was
the best president of the
United States.)

You can't argue that George
Washington wasn't the first
president. He was—it's a fact.
But you can argue that he
was the best, and use other
facts (He established the first
cabinet of advisors; he personally led a militia to stop
the Whiskey Rebellion; he gave the first Thanksgiving
proclamation) to support your opinion. If someone is

Be curious—learning is something you'll be doing your whole life.

arguing their opinion, they should use facts to support it. But no one should be arguing about facts, because they are what they are. Learning to recognize when someone is presenting their opinion as fact is a key element of critical thinking.

3. BE OPEN TO CHANGE

Thinking critically doesn't just apply to arguments and assumptions you hear from others—you should also be evaluating your own thinking, especially before you get into a debate in the first place! It takes effort and practice, but try to set aside some time each day to consider why you do (or think) the things you do. You might be surprised at what you figure out, and it could lead you to make some positive changes in your life!

PICK A SIDE!

An argument that justifies itself only through its own factless assumptions is an example of "circular reasoning" or (if you want to get really fancy) "tautology." An example of this would be: "You have to go to bed now because now it's bedtime." A better, non-circular version of this argument would be: "You have to go to bed now, otherwise you'll be tired and grumpy in the morning."

HOW TO WRITE A LETTER

ANT TO SHOW someone you really care? Put down the phone, get some paper and a pen and start writing a heartfelt message.

1. *THINK BEFORE YOU WRITE*

Unlike texting or email, writing a letter by hand means you have to carefully plan what you want to communicate before you start composing your message. There's no "delete" button in real life! Before you begin, make a list on a separate piece of paper (or on your phone) of everything you want to put in the letter.

John Wayne in *Flying Leathernecks* (1951).

2. OPENING IT UP

Even for informal letters between friends, you want to stick to a basic, tried-and-true format that's easy to follow. Start out the letter with a one-line greeting: "Dear _____," but if you're good friends with the recipient, you can also go with language that's a little less stiff, such as "Hi ___!"

3. GO WITH THE FLOW

There's no rule on how long or short the letter should be, but you want to make sure you are writing in complete paragraphs. Each paragraph should express a complete thought on a single subject so the reader can easily follow your train of thought. Don't jump from topic to topic within the same paragraph, and don't try to cram together a bunch of different ideas on the same topic. If you have something new to say, keep things simple by starting a new paragraph.

4. CLOSE IT UP

When finishing the letter, you want to end it on a word or phrase that gets its own line, and then the name of the recipient goes directly under that line. "Best wishes" "Your friend" or even "Sincerely" are all great options here. Just go with what feels natural!

HOW TO THANK A VETERAN

HOW YOUR GRATITUDE to the men and women willing to pay the ultimate price to preserve our freedoms.

1. *KEEP IT SIMPLE*

One of the best ways to thank a veteran is by doing just that—say "thank you" to a veteran! They tend to hear this a lot, so you may not notice an immediate impact. But even if they don't show it, you almost certainly helped brighten a veteran's day by speaking up. It's the right thing to do.

You can also show your gratitude with a smile and a warm gesture.

2. LEARN TO LISTEN

If the veteran is someone you know and feel comfortable talking to, ask them to talk a little about their service. Ask them about their uniform or their favorite part about serving their country. If they're wearing medals, ask them what they mean. You can also let the veteran drive the conversation. It's their story to share, and if they seem like they don't have much to say, simply say thank you again to let them know you care.

3. GIVE YOUR TIME

You don't have to limit your "thank you" to just words. If you feel passionate about showing your appreciation for our country's veterans, there are plenty of organizations that help support them at home and abroad. Pick one you like and see if there are volunteer opportunities for you!

TOP VETERANS ORGANIZATIONS

Whether you choose to donate money or your time, you'll be doing a great service by helping the cause of these organizations.

Homes For Our Troops

This organization builds and donates custom homes to injured veterans across the country.

K9s For Warriors

This organization provides service dogs to veterans in need. Additionally, many of the dogs are rescued from shelters.

Project Sanctuary

Helping veterans as well as their families with mental health needs, this organization is always seeking volunteers.

Operation Gratitude

Hosting birthday fundraisers and welcoming donations including cell phones and vehicles, this organization aims to show gratitude to veterans in as many ways as possible.

HOW TO KICK A BAD HABIT

 F YOU SEEM to keep doing something you no longer want to (or should) do, there are a few tips that'll help you cut back or quit altogether. It may take time, so be patient with yourself.

1. *WRITE DOWN WHY*

You'll need lots of motivation to break a bad habit, and summoning that willpower will require you to remind yourself why you're putting yourself through this change and discomfort in the first place. Take the time to write a short paragraph or bulleted list outlining the reasons you want to drop your habit and how much better life will be for you without it. Keep this handy so you can remind yourself why you wanted to quit in the first place when you feel tempted to revert back to your old ways.

Bad Habits
1.
2.
3.
4.
5.

2. *AVOID YOUR TRIGGERS*

Willpower is important, but it's also a limited resource, especially on days where you feel more stressed out than usual. Pick your battles by avoiding situations that trigger your bad habit. If you're trying to eat less  junk food, for example, that means not keeping bags of chips around the house. You probably can't avoid every scenario, but cutting down on these temptations as much as possible gives you a better chance at success.

3. *FORGIVE YOURSELF FOR BACKSLIDING*

You'll likely—OK, make that certainly—give in at some point and indulge in your bad habit. It happens. But as long as you don't give up on your goal of quitting it entirely, that's what matters. The road to a better you isn't a straight one and it will be filled with setbacks, but the important thing is you keep going toward your destination. The new and improved you will be worth it.

HOW TO FOLD AN AMERICAN FLAG

AKE SURE YOU know the proper way to handle the stars and stripes so you can show the flag the same respect you'd give the country it represents.

1. *FROM BOTTOM TO TOP*

Lay the flag flat on a table. With the flag facing toward you, fold it in half evenly from the bottom up. The striped section should completely cover the blue section with stars (called the Union).

2. *ANOTHER FOLD*

Take this new bottom edge and fold it to the top edge once again. Now the Union and the stripes should both be showing. Make sure the creases are tight and the corners line up with each other.

3. *TERRIFIC TRIANGLES*

Take the bottom-right corner of the striped edge and fold it down diagonally so that it meets the top edge. You should now have a triangle. Take the bottom-right corner of this triangle and fold it to the left, parallel to the bottom edge. Now you've made another triangle.

4. *FINAL FOLDS*

Keep folding this triangle toward the left until the entire flag ends up as one big triangle. This will usually take two folds parallel to the bottom edge, two parallel to the top edge and two more parallel to the bottom edge.

5. *ALL TUCKED IN*

Create a new triangle to tuck the remainder of the flag into the pocket your folding created in the previous step. Congratulations, you've folded up Old Glory like a true patriot!

HOW TO APOLOGIZE

HERE'S MORE TO owning up to a mistake than just saying "sorry." If you want to add more meaning to that word, you'll have to dig deeper. Here's how to deliver an apology that matters.

1. *TAKE YOUR TIME*

Depending on the nature of your mistake, you might want to let the other person cool off a bit and process things before you apologize. Doing this also gives you a chance to reflect on what exactly it was you did wrong and how you can do better. Still—if you know you're sorry for something you said or did in the moment, you can defuse further anger or frustration by stating your apology and asking for forgiveness.

The person you hurt might need time before accepting your apology.

2. DON'T BEAT AROUND THE BUSH

One of the most common mistakes people make when apologizing is still trying to justify their actions. Don't hedge your admission of wrongdoing with phrases such as, "I'm sorry you were offended," or "If I hurt your feelings, I'm sorry." An honest apology isn't conditional, and the fault does not lie with the person you wronged. Suck it up and say what you did was wrong without any qualifications or excuses.

GET SPECIFIC

Avoid a general apology ("I'm sorry"), which feels pretty empty. Tell the person exactly what it was you did wrong ("I'm sorry I forgot your birthday").

3. PROMISE TO BE BETTER (AND FOLLOW THROUGH)

After telling the other person you're sorry for what you did, let them know how you'll try to avoid making the same mistake in the future. Be as specific as possible about your plan to be better ("I'm sorry I forgot your birthday, and I'll set up a reminder on my phone so it doesn't happen again"). Then ensure you stick to your word, otherwise your next apology won't mean as much.

HOW TO BE A GOOD PUBLIC SPEAKER

ALKING TO LARGE groups is some people's biggest fear. It's perfectly natural to feel this way, and it's possible to overcome. Here's how to power through.

1. *PRACTICE MAKES PERFECT*

There's no shortcut to excellence: If you want to improve your public speaking, you need to practice as much as you can. If you have a speech prepared ahead of time (this is actually rule #1, whenever possible), recite it out loud to a friend or parent numerous times before the big day. Pay attention to the parts of the speech that trip you up and go over them repeatedly until you can recite the entire thing without error. Even if you don't have a planned speech to give, you can improve your public speaking skills by telling a story or joke or even by describing your surroundings to a trusted, patient friend or family member. The more you speak, the better you'll be at it!

2. *TAKE IT EASY*

You aren't likely to be in any physical danger when talking to a crowd, but that doesn't mean your nerves won't try to get the best of you. Worry and fear can cause you to either clam up completely or start speaking a mile a minute, neither of which is great for your audience. One way to build confidence and settle the butterflies in your stomach is to pretend you're addressing a friend instead of a crowd of strangers.

3. *STAND UP STRAIGHT AND LOOK 'EM IN THE EYE*

A good public speech doesn't just depend on what you say but how you say it. That means in addition to talking at a steady pace and not mumbling, you need to look the part of a confident speaker. Stand up straight, avoid shuffling your feet or fidgeting and make eye contact with different members of your audience as you go. Don't worry, it'll be over before you know it—and if you follow these steps, you'll deliver a speech they'll remember fondly long after you step away from the podium.

HOW TO APPRECIATE DIFFERENT CULTURES

IT'S A BIG WORLD out there, filled with people from all different walks of life. Here's how you can broaden your horizons and learn more about cultures that are different from your own!

1. *HIT THE BOOKS*

One of the best ways to deepen your understanding of another culture is by familiarizing yourself with its art and history. Try reading a book written by a famous author from that culture or watching a movie made by a well-regarded director. While works of fiction are always great, you should also learn something about the history of that culture to better understand the events that shaped it.

Read about different cultures

Differences should be celebrated, not discouraged.

2. GET FRIENDLY

There's no substitute for genuine friendship when it comes to appreciating a culture that's different from your own. If you already have a friend from a different culture, take the time to ask them questions you might have about traditions or holidays they celebrate that you aren't familiar with. Keep an open mind and listen more than you talk.

3. STAY RESPECTFUL

One rule you should always keep in mind when appreciating a different culture is to stay respectful of its traditions and beliefs, even if you don't necessarily understand them. Always treat others with respect and ensure whatever questions you ask are coming from a place of curiosity rather than judgment.

FOOD FOR THOUGHT

A great way to learn about another culture is to try its cuisine. You might even find your new favorite food!

HOW TO MAKE A POSITIVE IMPACT

HE WORLD HAS plenty of problems, but things won't get better if all you do is complain. Here's how you can help make positive changes that will make life better for everyone.

1. *PICK YOUR PASSION*

No matter which cause is dear to your heart, there are many ways you can help: The hardest part might be picking what activity you dedicate yourself to first. Since making a positive impact takes hard work, first make sure you truly care about what you're doing. If you hate working in the dirt, for example, volunteering to help out at a community garden might not be a good idea. By choosing a cause that lets you do an activity you love, you can make the world a better place and enjoy yourself at the same time!

Even if an activity seems small, it can make a big impact.

2. *KEEP IT CONSISTENT*

Nobody's going to look down their nose at you performing the occasional good deed, but to really make a difference it's best to stick with a routine others can count on. Your time is a precious resource, so think long and hard before you put it toward your good cause. People would rather have you make a less time-consuming commitment that you actually follow through on than to be disappointed by you not showing up despite your promises.

3. *PASS IT ON*

One of the beautiful things about doing good in the world is how it inspires others to do their part. Let the people in your life know how you're helping and what they can do if they want to join in. You don't have to be obnoxious about this and bring it up in every conversation, but don't be shy about your work, either!

WAYS TO MAKE AN IMPACT

Here's a starting point to help you decide how you can help make the world a better place.

- Start (or help at) a community garden
- Read to the elderly
- Tutor other students in a school subject you love
- Donate old toys or clothes
- Pick up litter at your local park
- Volunteer at an animal shelter
- Help out at a soup kitchen or food bank

John Wayne plays a game of chess on the set of *The War Wagon* (1967).

FUN & GAMES

MAKE TIME FOR FUN WITH THESE CLASSIC PASTIMES AND LEISURELY PURSUITS

HOW TO PLAY SOLITAIRE

 OU DON'T NEED a phone to keep yourself occupied—just a deck of playing cards and the know-how to play solitaire. And you can get the latter right here.

1. GOAL OF THE GAME

In classic solitaire, the goal of the game is to create four "foundation" piles of cards—one for each suit—with each pile laid out in ascending order from ace (the lowest) to king (the highest).

2. BUILD YOUR FIRST ROW

To begin, take a shuffled deck of 52 cards (no jokers) and deal the first card from the top of the deck so it lays faceup. Then, deal six more cards facedown so that they form a row with the faceup card (which is at the left end of the row).

3. ROW NUMBER TWO

Now deal another card faceup, laying it so it overlaps with the first card in the row that's facedown. Then deal five more cards facedown, each of them overlapping with the rest of the cards in the row.

4. REPEAT UNTIL DONE

Keep repeating this pattern of dealing a faceup card that overlaps the leftmost facedown card and then dealing facedown cards that overlap with the rest of the cards in the row. When you're done, it should look like the illustration below.

Put the cards you have left over in the deck off to the side and keep them handy—when you're out of moves, you'll have to draw more cards from this pile.

5. TAKE A LOOK

Look at the cards you've dealt faceup. Remember, the goal of the game is to build four suited foundation piles that count up from ace to king. If you see an ace, you should move it away from the cards in play since it's the start of a foundation pile.

6. *MAKE YOUR MOVES*

After you've moved any aces to start their own foundation piles, you can now start moving cards around—but there are rules. You can move a faceup card from its current pile to overlap the bottom card of a different pile only if :

• the two cards are different colors (red and black) and;
• the card being moved is exactly one value less than the card that will be directly above it on the pile.

So, for example, you could move the 4 of clubs (black) onto the pile where the bottom card is the 5 of hearts (red).

When moving cards to different piles, keep in mind the bottom card of each pile has to be turned faceup. And remember: whenever the bottom card of a pile can be added to one of your foundation piles, make sure you do so!

7. *KEEP AT IT*

As you play your available moves, you may find one of your piles is absorbed completely by the other piles. Keep that space blank! If you uncover a king card, you can move it to the blank space to create a new pile and potentially give yourself more moves.

If you ever find yourself out of moves, you can deal a card from the deck to see if it fits anywhere. If it does, great! If not, you must put that card into a separate "waste" pile and draw again from the deck. Keep doing this and making moves with your piles until you either deal all of the remaining cards from the deck (in which case you lose) or you successfully build the four foundation piles. Good luck!

VARIATIONS ON THE GAME
Here are some alternate ways to play solitaire.

Harder:

When you need to draw a card from the deck, instead deal three, faceup. You can only use the top card. If you can play the top card, you can play the next card (then the next). If you can't use the card that's faceup, you deal from the deck again—dealing three cards. This variation makes solitaire much harder!

Easier:

When you reach the end of the deck but still aren't finished building all four foundational piles, shuffle the cards you discarded and start over.

HOW TO READ AND WRITE IN CODE

EXT TIME YOU and a pal want to share a secret, you can get a little more creative than simply exchanging text messages. Try using one of these codes that will have others scratching their heads.

1. *THE REVERSE ALPHABET*

This code's pretty simple, but sometimes simple is what the job calls for. For this code, substitute one letter in the alphabet for another. In this case, "Z" means "A", "Y" means "B" and so on. Here's the code written out:

Plain Alphabet

| A | B | C | D | E | F | G | H | I | J | K | L | M | N | O | P | Q | R | S | T | U | V | W | X | Y | Z |

Coded Alphabet

| Z | Y | X | W | V | U | T | S | R | Q | P | O | N | M | L | K | J | I | H | G | F | E | D | C | B | A |

If you wanted to write **"Howdy, pilgrim!"** in this code, it would read:

"Sldwb, krotirn!"

2. *CAESAR CIPHER*

This code's been around for a while—it was supposedly used by Julius Caesar around 100 B.C.E. It's stuck around for a reason and gives you a lot of flexibility in creating your own code. Like the reverse alphabet code, this cipher involves substituting one letter of the alphabet for another. But this time, you're shifting the alphabet a couple of places left or right depending on what you want. How do you move an alphabet? Like so:

Plain Alphabet

| A | B | C | D | E | F | G | H | I | J | K | L | M | N | O | P | Q | R | S | T | U | V | W | X | Y | Z |

Coded Alphabet

| Y | Z | A | B | C | D | E | F | G | H | I | J | K | L | M | N | O | P | Q | R | S | T | U | V | W | X |

See what we did there? We moved the alphabet right by two spaces. Writing in this code, "Y" means "A" and "A" means "C." So if you want to write to a friend "Meet me at the tree," in this code, it would look like:

Kccr kc yr rfc rpcc

3. *PIGPEN CODE*

If you and your friend really want a code that's tough to crack, look no further than the pigpen code. This one's a little advanced, so don't feel bad if it takes you a few tries before you master it. But once you do, your secrets will be safer than gold in a bank vault. Let's take a look at what the code looks like:

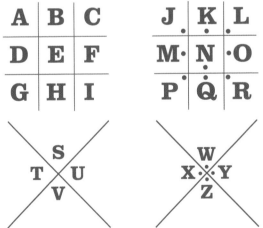

The written code depends on you and your friend recognizing which of the shapes formed by the lines and dots are paired with which letter. "A", for example, is written as ⌐, while "J" is written as ⌐. Writing "Hey there!" in pigpen code would look like this:

HOW TO PITCH A BASEBALL

 HERE'S A LOT OF fun to be found in baseball, but few things compare with striking out a batter with a well-thrown pitch. Learn how to bring the heat and be the hero for your team!

1. HOLD ON

You can't pitch without knowing how to master the different grips used for different situations. Some of the most common include:

Two-Seam Fastball

Grasp the baseball along with the seams with your index and middle fingers while your thumb and your ring finger cradle the ball on its sides. To add more speed, go with the four-seam fastball. That requires holding the ball with your index and middle fingers so they are just a little over the laces of the ball.

Curveball

Hold the ball along the seams with your index and middle fingers, keeping them together tightly.

Changeup

Make an "OK" sign with your thumb and index finger and place those fingers on the side of the ball. Your other fingers should grasp the baseball.

Knuckleball

Grab the ball by the sides with your thumb and ring finger, digging your nails into the ball and using your index and middle fingers to hold the top. Bend these two fingers so your knuckles stick out in the air.

2. FANCY FOOTWORK

Stand with your feet shoulder-width apart, holding the ball with your dominant hand placed inside your glove so the batter can't see what grip you're using and anticipate which pitch is coming! Face the catcher with your toes pointed straight at them.

3. THE WINDUP...

Take a small step back with your left foot (if you're right-handed) and shift your weight to your left leg. Now pivot on the ball of your right foot so it is parallel to the catcher. Bring your left leg up until your thigh is parallel to the ground.

4. ...AND THE PITCH!

Now extend your left leg toward the catcher, taking a big step while your right (now back) foot kicks up to provide power—you can put speed on or off the ball by how aggressively you step and twist. At the same time, bring your arms downward with the back arm (which is holding the ball) nearly perpendicular to the ground. Now bring that arm in an arc toward the catcher, timing it so that the arm is extended completely at the same time the left leg hits the ground.

HOW TO CARE FOR A PET

O MATTER WHAT kind of creature or critter you call your pet, taking care of it is a big responsibility! Here are some general tips on how to make sure you're doing right by your animal buddy.

1. *NOT A TOY*

The most important piece of advice to remember is that your pet is a living creature that depends on you and not a toy you can just ignore when you're bored with it. There'll be plenty of times when you have to pay attention to your pet when you'd rather be doing something else, but that's part of being a responsible owner. If that sounds like too much hassle (And there's nothing wrong with thinking that!), then you aren't ready for a pet right now.

2. FOOD AND SHELTER

Whether a kitten, lizard, dog or hissing cockroach, your pet will need the basics of food, water and someplace safe to live. The specifics of how often you need to provide food and water (and what kind of shelter is needed) varies from pet to pet, but make sure you and your parents figure this out before you bring the pet home.

John Wayne with a canine companion, c. 1950s.

There's also a good chance your pet doesn't know how to use the toilet when you first meet them, so be prepared to clean up after them and potty train or accommodate them if possible.

3. PAY ATTENTION

Keep an eye out for any changes of behavior or appearance in your pet. Is it turning into a chonk? Consider exercising with it more or cutting back how much you feed it. Does it seem tired and like it doesn't want to move? It might be time to take it to the veterinarian to make sure it isn't sick. Remember, your pet isn't able to tell you what it needs or what's wrong with it using words, but many are able to communicate in other ways. It's up to you to pay attention to what's going on and read the signs.

HOW TO TRAIN A DOG

HEY MAY BE man's best friend, but dogs need a little guidance to help them fit in with the family. Here's where to start.

1. *POSITIVE ATTITUDE*

When you begin training your dog, it won't understand basic commands such as "sit" or "stay," so you need to use treats to show your dog what actions you want it to perform. This means you'll have to get a little creative when it comes to teaching your dog what actions earn it a reward. For example, one way to teach a dog to obey "sit" is by putting a treat right in front of its nose and then raising the treat above the dog's head. When the dog puts its bottom on the floor—in other words, when it sits—give it the treat. Keep repeating this, and eventually start saying "sit" before the dog sits down to get it to understand that when you say sit and it puts its rump on the floor, that's a good thing.

John Wayne plays with his dogs at home, c. 1952.

2. *KEEP IT BITE-SIZED*
You may think longer training sessions will quickly bring your dog up to speed, but it's actually the opposite. Dogs benefit from short, 5-to-10-minute training sessions spread throughout the day. Each session should focus on just one command, and remember to be patient—it can take 4 or 5 weeks for things to really sink in.

3. *QUIET THEN LOUD*
It's usually best to start training your dog in a familiar, quiet room in your home. But once your dog gets down the basics of the command, you should then move the training to someplace that has more distractions, like your yard or a park. Don't be shocked if your dog initially does worse out there with all the distractions—it will eventually get back into the swing of things, and you'll avoid having a dog that's obedient in the house but completely wild when out in the world.

HOW TO HUNT FOR FOSSILS

OSSILS ARE THE remains of ancient life that has been preserved in rock, and they can be anything from a dinosaur skeleton to a flower. Sounds cool, right? Here's how to find some.

1. LIKE A ROCK

For something to become a fossil, it must first become buried under layers of sediment (such as dirt or sand) that build up over at least 10,000 years. That's why sedimentary rocks such as limestone, mudstone or shale often contain fossils, since these rocks are formed from layers of sediment coming together over time. Looking for sedimentary rocks around riverbeds or near bodies of water can be a good tactic for finding fossils, since it's more likely the remains of small aquatic life ended up in a rock!

Look closely— they could be blending in with the environment.

2. *KEEP YOUR EYES PEELED*

Finding fossils means keeping an eye out for anything that looks out of the ordinary when examining rocks. You're looking for the outlines of a shell, plant or even footprints. Depending on how old the rock is and how exposed it is to the elements, the fossil may be very faint. So make sure you look at the rocks carefully and bring a magnifying glass to help you spot hard-to-see fossils.

3. *GO TO A MUSEUM*

Since you're unlikely to find the fossil of a T-Rex in your backyard, many museums around the country have impressive collections of dinosaur bones and other fossil types for you to study up close! Plan a trip to a natural history museum to see for yourself.

T-Rex Skull

HOW TO SEND MESSAGES IN MORSE CODE

HEN YOU WANT TO communicate but can't risk writing anything down, you can rely on Morse code to help. It may seem tricky at first, but with a little practice, you'll be a master in no time. Here's how it works!

1. *SOUNDING OFF AND LIGHTING UP*

Morse code was invented in the 19th century by Samuel F.B. Morse, a portrait painter who conceived of the idea after learning about the invention of the electromagnet. Morse code allows for communication across vast distances using the telegraph. Telegraph wires couldn't transmit voices, but they could carry a simple beeping sound that was generated by electricity. Morse code lets people send messages using this sound by assigning each letter of the alphabet a unique combination of short sounds (known as "dits") and longer sounds (known as "dahs").

Plus, you don't need a telegraph to send signals in Morse code. You could clap or hum a message in Morse code, or bang on a drum. Additionally, dits and dahs don't have to be limited to sounds—you can signal in Morse code by flashing a flashlight! A quick flash works like a dit, while a longer flash is a dah.

2. *A MATTER OF TIMING*

To use Morse code, you have to follow some basic rules about timing—otherwise the person on the receiving end of your message won't know when one letter or word begins and ends. When sending a message, keep the following in mind:
- A dit is the signal that lasts the least amount of time.
- A dah equals the length of three dits.
- The space you leave between dits and dahs when

signaling a letter (for example, — . — or "K") is equal to one dit.

- The space you leave when you are done with one letter and move on to the next is equal to three dits.
- The space you leave when you are done with an entire word and are ready to start signaling the next is equal to seven dits.

Because the amount of time you spend not signaling tells the message's recipient whether you are in the middle of signaling a letter or a whole new word, you have to stick to your rhythm for your message to make sense. Make sure you know what you want to signal before you begin—it helps to write your coded message down so you can use it as a reference as you send your signal.

3. *HOW TO SPELL*

Here's how to signal each letter of the alphabet (and some other helpful info!) using today's Morse code. A dot stands for a dit, while a dash represents a dah.

MORSE CODE

A	.—	N	—.	1	.————
B	—...	O	———	2	..———
C	—.—.	P	.——.	3	...——
D	—..	Q	——.—	4	....—
E	.	R	.—.	5	.....
F	..—.	S	...	6	—....
G	——.	T	—	7	——...
H	....	U	..—	8	———..
I	..	V	...—	9	————.
J	.———	W	.——	0	—————
K	—.—	X	—..—	@	.——.—.
L	.—..	Y	—.——		
M	——	Z	——..		

HOW TO FOLD THE PERFECT PAPER AIRPLANE

 UST ABOUT ANYONE can make a basic paper airplane, but we'll teach you how to make a cutting-edge model that will soar through the sky as if piloted by one of Duke's characters.

1. Fold your paper in half vertically, then unfold it.

2. Fold down each of the upper corners to the center of the paper. You should have a big triangle at the top of your paper now.

3. Fold down the tip of the triangle to the center of the paper.

4. Fold what are now the two upper sides down toward the center and make sure to crease the edges.

5. Flip the paper (which is a big triangle at this point) and fold the bottom corners to the center. Crease the edges.

6. Fold the right and left sides down toward the center, but leave about ⅛-inch of paper from the bottom undisturbed. Use a ruler to measure if you need to.

7. Fold the entire paper in half vertically.

8. Fold down your wing, starting the fold about a quarter of the way from the top of the plane. Then turn the plane over and repeat to create your second wing.

9. Where the two triangles meet at the center of the plane's bottom, fold in about 1 inch from the center to create an inner flap on both sides.

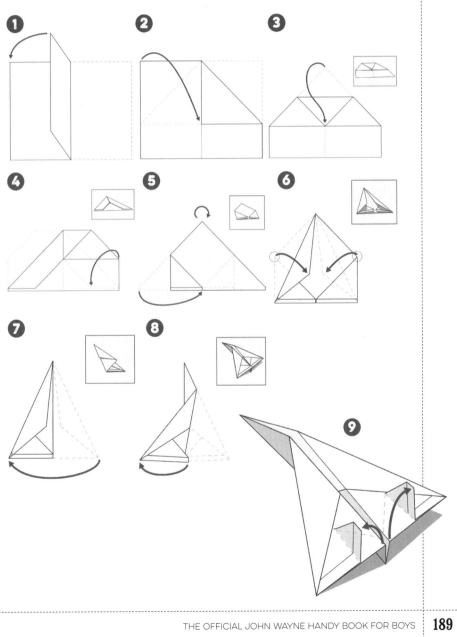

HOW TO IDENTIFY INSECTS

CIENTISTS BELIEVE THERE are around 10 quintillion insects in the world. That's 10,000,000,000,000,000,000 ants, roaches, flies and more. But not every creepy-crawly critter you see is an insect. Learn how to sort 'em out!

1. *GET A CLOSER LOOK*

Most insects are teeny-tiny, but even the big ones can benefit from a closer look if you're trying to identify them. A magnifying glass is a great tool for examining insects in the wild without having to get eye-to-compound-eye with them. Just make sure to use the magnifying glass to look at insects and not to harm them.

2. *KEEP YOUR HANDS TO YOURSELF*

While most insects and other bugs are harmless, some can bite or sting. Try to remain hands-off when you're inspecting bugs, for their safety and yours.

3. *KNOW YOUR PARTS*

Once you've got a good look at a bug, you can start looking for the things that identify it as an insect! Every insect will have

Know Your Parts

- A head, which contains eyes, mouthparts and (usually) two antennae
- A middle segment of their body called the thorax, where three pairs of legs are attached
- A bottom section called an abdomen
- A hard outer shell called an exoskeleton

Insects will also often have a pair of wings, though that's not true for every species. And in species that do have wings, sometimes only males or females have them—male ants, for example, have wings while females don't.

4. INSECT OR NOT?
Now let's see if you can put your book smarts to good use. Which of the following is an insect?

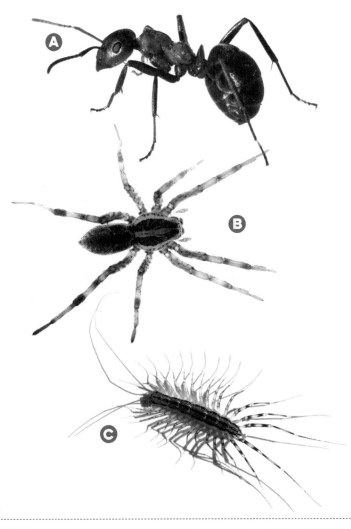

HOW TO PLANT A GARDEN

OOKING FOR A REASON to play around in the dirt? Look no further than a chance to develop your green thumb.

1. *PICK YOUR SPOT*

The first step in planting a garden is to find a good location. Ideally, you want someplace where it won't be a pain for you to water and that also receives plenty of sunlight throughout the day. Try to find someplace that has weeds or grass growing there already, as that's a sign that the soil is able to nourish living things! Once you've found the site of your future garden, you can place a small "bed" there. An old sandbox works great if you have one, but buying a simple garden bed (or better yet, making your own out of wood) will also work.

Don't be afraid to get your hands (and clothes) dirty.

2. SELECT YOUR SOIL

Once you have a garden bed, you can start filling it with soil that will nourish your plants! It turns out dirt isn't just dirt—experienced gardeners try and use different types of soil to help grow different types of plants. But for now, you should be fine mixing 2 to 3 inches of topsoil (you can buy this from your local gardening shop) with about 8 inches of soil that you can dig up from your gardening site.

3. PLANT YOUR SEEDS

Now decide what you want to grow and find the appropriate seeds at your local plant nursery or gardening store. Once you have your seeds, go out to the garden and dig a shallow trench with your fingers. Lay the seeds in a line in the trench, leaving space between them. Then cover the trench in soil and get ready to nurture your baby plants to life.

4. TAKE CARE

Gardens usually like an inch of rain each week, but the weather doesn't always cooperate. That's why you need to water your garden every few days if it doesn't rain. Try to water your garden early in the day, and make sure you take the time to get the soil nice and moist. Soon, your garden should be flourishing!

HOW TO MAKE AN UNDERWATER VIEWER

 ANT TO TAKE A peek at what's going on below the surface of that stream or lake? Here's how to uncover underwater secrets without getting soaked.

1. GATHER YOUR SUPPLIES

To get started, you (or an adult) will need to gather the following items:

| A CAN OPENER | A METAL CAN at least 4 inches in diameter (Coffee cans work great!) | CLEAR HEAVY-DUTY PLASTIC WRAP | 2 THICK RUBBER BANDS |

2. BOTTOMS OFF

Cut the top and bottom off your can opener so that you have a metal tube open on both ends. Ask an adult to help you use pliers to crimp down the edges of the opening you made—that way you won't cut yourself on sharp metal!

3. PLASTICS MAKE IT POSSIBLE
Now take some of your plastic wrap and stretch it across the bottom of the can so it completely covers the opening. Use the two rubber bands to secure the plastic, and make sure it's stretched tight enough so it makes a waterproof seal.

4. GO FOR A DIP
With your viewer in hand, go find a body of water you want to study and place the viewer under the water, plastic end first. You should be able to look straight through the plastic and clearly see what's going on underwater, no bathing suit required. Just remember not to wander too far from the shoreline when looking for a place to observe.

HOW TO IDENTIFY ROCKS

N **OT ALL STONES** are created equal. Some contain precious minerals like gold, while others can be used to power a city! Here's how you can identify some of the most common rocks around.

1. *KNOW YOUR TYPE*

It's time for a little science lesson! Rocks can be broken down into three basic types:

Igneous rocks form when hot magma cools enough so it turns into a solid.

Sedimentary rocks form from all the soil, minerals, plant and animal remains that join together over a long period of time. This is happening even now!

Metamorphic rocks form when either an igneous or sedimentary rock is exposed to a great amount of heat, pressure or hot minerals.

Unless you live near a volcano, you probably will run into sedimentary rocks the most. Here are some of the cooler ones for you to spot!

Depending on the area, you might find an interesting mix.

FLINT

You can usually find these rocks around streams or riverbeds. They have a waxy, smooth surface that's almost like glass. Flint is  usually either black or dark gray. One way to test if a rock is flint is by asking an adult to strike it with a knife made of carbon steel—if it's flint, you should see sparks flying!

LIMESTONE

Despite its name, this stone is neither green nor juicy. But it is often full of fantastic fossils! Usually gray or white in color, limestone often forms from the remains of tiny little animals that live in the water. And because the bodies of bigger animals  (such as a bird or fish) sometime end up at the bottom of the water where the limestone is forming, those stones often contain fossils of all kinds of critters. Spooky!

CONGLOMERATE

Found at the bottom of bodies of water, these look like a bunch of smaller, rounded rocks glued together in one big lump. And that's basically what they are! Conglomerates form when these different  types of rock fuse together with a kind of natural cement and then are rounded by friction from the water.

HOW TO PLAY CAPTURE THE FLAG

F YOU'RE LUCKY enough to have beautiful weather outside and a bunch of friends looking for some fun, then the stars might be aligning for an epic game of capture the flag. Learn how to play a game that's a test of teamwork, tenacity and tactics!

1. *SET UP YOUR SPACE*

While technically there's nothing stopping you from playing a game of capture the flag indoors, in practice it's pretty boring. A big part of the game's fun is romping through the great outdoors, so find yourself a big grassy field, a wooded area or anywhere that can accommodate you and your friends running around! Just make sure the play area doesn't have anything dangerous that could easily hurt you when you're running at full speed (like holes, lots of playground equipment, etc.) and let an adult know where you plan on playing.

2. *LAY DOWN SOME GROUND RULES*

The first premise of capture the flag is that each team has their own flag at their home base, which they can't move. The goal is to run over to the other team's base, take their flag and bring it back to your base. Each player can be "caught" by a player of the opposing team, after which they are out of the game (either for a short time or the rest of the game, depending on how you want to play).

Beyond that, you can play any way you want! Here are some recommendations to help everyone have a good time:

• An easy way to determine if a player is "caught" is by another player tagging them. But if you want to bring some equipment into the mix, the possibilities really open up. For instance, you could wear flags that the other player has to tear off you (like flag football) or even use squirt guns or foam weapons to "catch" players.

• Instead of having "caught" players sit out the rest of the game, make them do 10 jumping jacks before they can get back in the action. That keeps everyone involved while still giving players an incentive not to get nabbed!

• Make a rule that team members have to maintain a certain distance from their own flag—otherwise people might just wait around by their base, which makes for a less exciting game.

3. HAVE A STRATEGY

Now that you know how to play capture the flag, it's time to learn how to win! If everyone just rushes at the enemy team's flag, you might get lucky and eventually win. But it's smarter (and more fun) to make a plan. Get your team to agree on each member taking on one of three roles: defender, hunter and striker. Defenders generally stick closer to their own base and try to nab anyone going after their own flag. Hunters roam closer to enemy territory but are focused on capturing and distracting enemy team members. And strikers are those who try to make a beeline for the enemy flag to bring back to base. Good luck!

HOW TO MAKE AN ERUPTING VOLCANO

ERE'S HOW YOU can pretend to master one of Mother Nature's most destructive forces while having fun. And don't worry—you won't burn the house down.

1. BUILD YOUR BASE

Take a cardboard box and cut off the top so that you're left with an open cardboard square. Now place an empty plastic bottle in the center of the cardboard with the opening pointing upward (make sure the cap is off).

2. FIND YOUR FRAME

Take some newspaper and mold it around the bottle so everything but the opening is covered in one layer. Next, use strips of tape to secure this first layer of newspaper to the bottle by having the tape run from the opening of the bottle down the sides of the paper. Use plenty of tape! When you're done, this will be the frame on which you'll pile even more paper.

3. BUILD IT UP

Take more newspaper and dip it in your papier-mâché mixture, then start molding it around the frame. Feel free to make your volcano as large as you like, but just remember to leave an opening up top! When you're done, you should have a volcano-shaped pile of newspaper. Wait for the papier-mâché to dry before moving on to the next step.

4. MAKE IT COLORFUL

While your volcano might have the right shape, it still looks like newspaper. Fix that by painting it brown for a realistic-looking mountain, with some red around the top to represent lava. But if you don't care about realism, feel free to paint the volcano however you want! Once you're done, wait until the paint dries.

5. TIME FOR 'SPLOSIONS

Now for the really fun part: Using a funnel, pour about 3 teaspoons of baking soda down the opening at the top of the volcano. Then add about half a glass of warm water that's mixed with some drops of red food dye. When you're ready for the fireworks, add about a glassful of vinegar and watch the "lava" erupt!

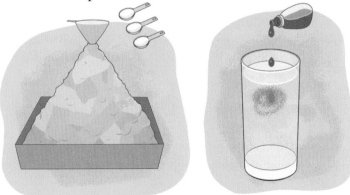

HOW TO IDENTIFY PATTERNS IN THE STARS

HOUSANDS OF YEARS ago, people looked at the night sky and found patterns in the stars. These groups of stars helped people make sense of the vast beauty of the heavens. Here's how you can identify some of the same constellations in your backyard!

1. *THE BIG DIPPER*

To find this asterism (a name for a star formation smaller than a constellation), you need to first face north (pg. 36) and then look at the sky. The Big Dipper's position changes depending on the time of year, but you should be able to spot a bright grouping of seven stars that looks like a bowl with a handle attached. During spring and summer, this constellation will be higher in the sky than in autumn and winter, when it's closer to the horizon.

2. *ORION THE HUNTER*

To locate this mighty warrior in the sky, look southwest (if you're in the Northern Hemisphere) for three bright stars in a line. This asterism is called Orion's Belt and forms part of the larger constellation. Above the belt are three stars in an upside-down "V", which represent Orion's head and shoulders (the ancients had great imaginations!). Straight above Orion's left "shoulder" are five stars that form his club. To

the right of Orion's right shoulder are six stars that form a crooked vertical line representing his shield.

3. *DRACO THE DRAGON*

One of the easiest ways to spot Draco is to find the Big Dipper and the North Star. You already know how to find the first, and finding the second is easy—just face north and look for the brightest star in the sky. Between the edge of the Big Dipper's bowl and the North Star, you should be able to spot another bright star that is the end of Draco's tail. Then it's just a matter of tracing Draco's body ending with his square-shaped head.

HOW TO PLAY CHESS

DON'T LET ITS nickname of "the game of kings" intimidate you—anyone can learn to play chess and, given how fun it is, everyone should. Here's what you need to know to get started on your journey toward becoming a grandmaster—or at least as good as John Wayne.

1. *SET 'EM UP*

Like checkers, chess is played by two people with a board made of 64 squares. Each player should have a white square at the bottom right—that's how you know the board is oriented correctly. It doesn't matter if you choose black or white—each player sets up their pieces (almost) the same way:

- The eight pawns (the smallest pieces) occupy the row second closest to the player.
- The two rooks (they usually look like castles) occupy the outside squares on either side of the board in the row closest to the player.
- Each of the two knights (horses) occupies the square next to the rook. Likewise, the bishops (long skinny pieces that aren't the king or queen) occupy the square next to the knights.
- For the king (his crown usually has a cross) and queen (her crown looks more angular), place the queen on the row's remaining square that's the same color as your pieces. So if

CHESS PIECES & HOW THEY MOVE

Once you familiarize yourself with the pieces and how they work,
you'll be well on your way to mastering "the game of kings."

PAWN

A pawn can move forward one square at a time with some exceptions. If an enemy piece is on the square directly in front of it, the pawn can't move forward to capture that piece. However, pawns can move one square diagonally to capture an enemy piece. If there's no enemy piece on the square to capture, pawns can't move diagonally. And just to make things even more confusing, you are allowed to move the pawn forward two squares the first time you move it in the game. Don't worry, it gets simpler from here!

ROOK

These pieces can move as many squares as you wish, vertically or horizontally, until you hit another piece. If it's your opponent's, you can take it.

KNIGHT

As a mounted warrior, the knight has a lot of mobility. Knights move either two squares horizontally and then one square vertically or two squares vertically and then one square horizontally. Unlike other pieces, knights can move "through" their own team's pieces (think of the knights as jumping from square to square, rather than marching like your other pieces).

BISHOP

The bishop can move diagonally as many squares as you want.

QUEEN

By far the most powerful piece on the board, the queen can move in any direction for as many squares as you want.

KING

The king can move in any direction, but only one square at a time.

you're playing black, the queen goes on the black square and the king goes on the white one (and if you're playing white, it's the opposite).

2. *COMMANDING YOUR ARMY*

In chess, the goal is to move your pieces to capture the enemy king. Along the way, you'll almost certainly have to capture other enemy pieces as well, which you do by moving one of your pieces to occupy the same square that an enemy piece sits on. Capturing an enemy piece ends the movement of your piece and ends your turn. Your turn also ends when you've finished moving one piece (whether you've captured an enemy piece or not). With the exception of knights, you can't move one of your pieces through another one of your pieces.

3. *HOW TO WIN*

While the technical goal of chess is to capture the enemy king, the rules of the game make it so what you're really doing is forcing the enemy king in a situation where he can't move without you being able to capture him on the next turn—a situation called "checkmate."

When you make a move that directly threatens the enemy king—in other words, if your opponent were to not move their king during their move then you could capture that king on your next move—you have to say "check." This lets your opponent know their king is in danger. Don't worry, they'll have to do the same for you!

4. *BASIC STRATEGY*

People have been playing chess for hundreds of years, a tradition that's led to a seemingly endless amount of strategies, tactics, tips and more. Part of the fun of playing chess is absorbing some of this knowledge and applying it to your own game, which you definitely should do! But for beginners, it's more helpful to keep the following in mind:

Take Your Time

While professional chess games set a time limit for each player's turn, there's no need to be so intense when starting out. Think about what move you want to make and what will change after you make that move. Which of your opponent's pieces do you now threaten? Are any of your pieces in danger now? How do you expect your opponent to react? These are the questions you need to answer before each move.

John Wayne on the set of *Circus World* (1964).

Move With Purpose

While your ultimate goal is to checkmate your opponent, you'll find that a game of chess consists of smaller objectives that are unique to every game. For example, if you have a powerful piece such as your queen surrounded by your own pieces, you'll need to figure out which of those pieces you should move in order to free her to attack your opponent's pieces. Every move you make should have a purpose, whether it's to capture an enemy piece, free up space for your own pieces or to defend against an enemy attack.

Offense and Defense

Building on the point above, you need to know when to use your move to set up an attack versus when to build up your defenses. The most common way to capture an enemy piece is by moving your pieces so that your opponent will lose one of their pieces no matter what move they make. Since both you and your opponent move your pieces one turn at a time, you may have to set up these traps several moves in advance.

To defend your pieces, you have to arrange it so that if your opponent captures one of your pieces, it means you'll capture a piece of theirs of equal or higher value on the next turn. While certain pieces are inherently more valuable than others (you have many more options when moving a queen versus moving a pawn, for example), how you define "value" also depends on the situation. Depending on how the game has developed, losing a pawn that's defending a specific square might kick off a chain of moves that ends in checkmate, for instance.

HOW TO INTERVIEW A GRANDPARENT

ITTING DOWN AND having a long talk with one of your elders isn't just a sign of respect—it can reveal stories you never suspected.

1. *LEARN ABOUT THE STORY OF YOU*
Grandparents aren't just good for old-fashioned candy and sending you money on your birthday. They also have plenty of stories about how the world was in the past, and (more importantly) all of the embarrassing things your mom or dad did when they were your age. Learning more about where you come from and the people you love is always worthwhile.

Be sure to take plenty of notes as you listen to their answers.

2. THINK OF SOME QUESTIONS

You probably know your grandparents pretty well (or maybe you don't, which is OK too!), but coming up with a list of questions to ask them will help keep the conversation flowing. Some examples of questions are:

- *Where were you born?*
- *What did you want to be when you grew up?*
- *Where did you grow up?*
- *What was your first job?*
- *How did you meet Grandma/Grandpa?*
- *What were your parents and grandparents like?*

3. FIND SOMEPLACE COMFORTABLE AND QUIET

You don't want to settle in for a long conversation in a noisy environment that makes it difficult for both of you to focus or hear each other. Find a quiet room with a few comfortable chairs or a couch you can settle in on, and maybe bring a snack or two. After all, this could take a while!

4. STAY ENGAGED

While you should have a list of questions to ask, you shouldn't feel restricted by them. As your grandparent starts talking, don't be afraid to ask follow-up questions to anything you hear that's interesting or that you don't understand. Just try to let them finish their thought first before launching into a new question—nobody likes being constantly interrupted, even if they do love you.

HOW TO MAKE AND WRITE WITH INVISIBLE INK

OT SOME SECRET info you need to share with a friend? You can hide the message in plain sight with the help of invisible ink. Here's how to whip up a batch of your own!

1. *MIX IT UP*

Head to the kitchen and get a small bowl and some baking soda. In the bowl, create a mixture of equal parts water and baking soda. There shouldn't be any undissolved baking soda in the bowl—if there is, add just a little more water until it all dissolves.

2. *GRAB YOUR UTENSIL*

Now that you have your ink ready, you'll need something to write with. A Q-tip, toothpick or anything of a similar shape and size should work. Dip one end in the bowl and then write out your message on a piece of white paper. Thicker paper, such as an index card, works better than flimsier paper that might get warped from the ink's wetness.

3. DRY IT OUT

Once you're done writing your message, wait for the ink to dry completely before touching the paper. If you're in a hurry, you can get a blow dryer, put it on a low heat setting and aim it at the paper to speed up the drying!

4. THE BIG REVEAL

If you want to uncover the hidden writing on your paper, you'll have to be prepared to get a little messy. Ask an adult to get you some frozen concentrated grape juice the next time they're at the grocery store (you can also try regular grape juice, but it may not work as well). Melt some of the grape juice concentrate in the microwave and pour it into a bowl. Now take a brush and paint the paper with a light coating of juice. The acid in the juice will react with the baking soda mixture and reveal your message. Voila!

HOW TO POP AN OLLIE LIKE A PRO

 KATEBOARDING ON ITS own is cool. Even cooler? When you start doing a few tricks with your deck. The ollie lets you launch yourself into the air, a helpful technique that serves as the foundation for future tricks.

1. *SAFETY FIRST*

There's no sugarcoating things—you're going to fall down a lot when learning to ollie. For that reason, you should practice on a patch of grass or someplace where the ground is soft. And you should always be wearing your helmet!

A good pair of skateboarding shoes can help you grip the board.

2. *FIND YOUR FOOTING*

Standing on your skateboard, your front foot should be placed in the middle of the board just behind the front truck bolts. Make sure your back foot is at the back tail of the board. Try to place the weight of your back foot on the ball of your foot, since this will help you perform the movement more smoothly.

3. *GET LOW TO SOAR HIGH*

Bend your knees so you're crouching, but don't feel the need to go too extreme here. While crouching as low as you can will maximize your airtime, it's also harder to control your balance. As a beginner, you should be fine with just a medium-sized crouch.

4. *KICK BACK AND SLIDE FORWARD*

Jump up from your crouched position, and at the same time kick down hard with your back foot while sliding your front foot forward toward the tip of the board. When sliding the front foot forward, make sure you're doing so with the edge of your foot and not the sole. And when kicking with the back foot, you want to make sure the back of the board has as little contact with the ground as possible—any dragging here will spell the end of your ollie. If you do this in one coordinated motion, then both you and your skateboard should fly into the air.

5. *STRAIGHTEN UP AND LAND SAFELY*

Awesome, you're in the air! When your sliding front foot reaches the end of the board, kick down with your front foot to help straighten the skateboard in the air and to bring it back to the ground. As the skateboard lands, try to have your front foot directly over the front trucks and your back foot over the back trucks—this will minimize the chance of you breaking the board when you land! Finally, bend your knees a little when the board makes contact to help absorb some shock.

HOW TO MAKE ROCK CANDY

HIS DELICIOUS TREAT may be hard, but it's easy as pie when you know what to do! Learn how to whip together your own batch of this spectacular sweet.

1. *THE SUPPLIES YOU'LL NEED*

SKEWERS	MASON JAR	CLOTHESPINS	POT OR PAN
WHITE SUGAR	TIN FOIL	FOOD COLORING	RUBBER BAND

2. *PREP WORK*

Take a skewer and run it under the faucet. Once it's wet, coat the skewer in white sugar and wait until it dries (it should take about an hour or so). Either before or after this step, make sure the skewer fits in your mason jar and that there's at least an inch of space between the end of the skewer and the bottom of the jar (you don't want the rock candy to grow on the jar, which makes the skewer difficult to remove). You can attach clothespins to the skewer, then balance them on top of the jar.

3. *STIR THINGS UP*

Fill a pan or pot with about 4 cups of water. Bring the water to a boil on the stovetop (ask an adult for help with this), then pour a cup of sugar into the water. Stir until the sugar is completely dissolved, then repeat the process with another cup of sugar. Remember to stir until the sugar dissolves—in the end, you should have a water-sugar solution. Remove the pan or pot from the heat, then stir in 2 to 3 drops of food coloring.

4. *POUR SOME SUGAR*
Take your water-sugar solution and pour it into the mason jar. Cover the opening of the jar with wax paper or tin foil and secure it with a rubber band. Poke the skewer through the hole so it's suspended in the water-sugar solution.

5. *WAIT AND SEE*
It takes about seven days for the rock candy crystals to grow. When your skewer is surrounded by big chunks of crystal deliciousness, remove the skewer (you'll have to wiggle it free of the hardened solution) and enjoy!

SAFE SNACKING
It's great to share the tasty treat you made, but you should ask an adult before giving rock candy to a younger child. It could be a choking hazard, or for some kids, too much sugar!

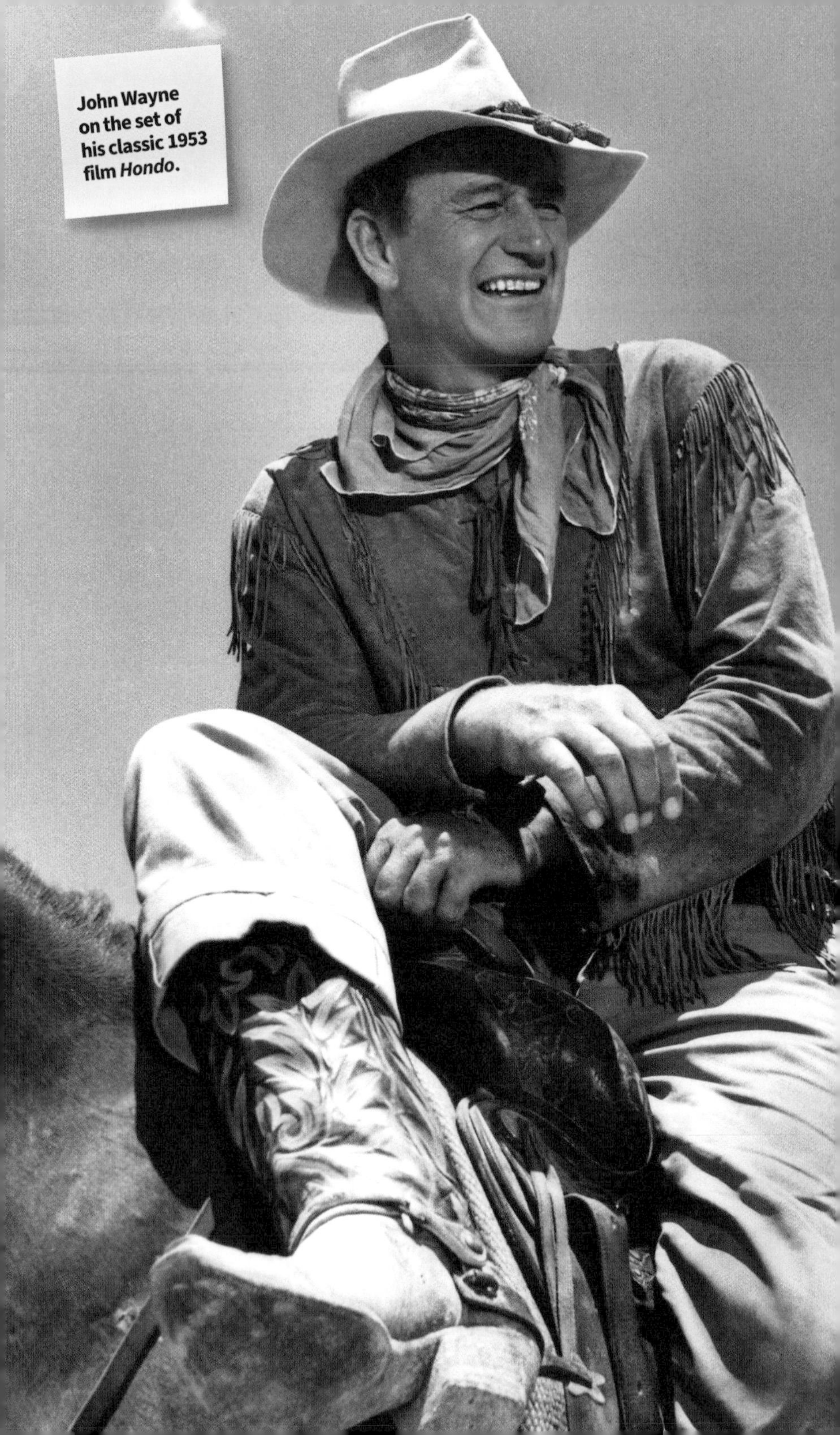

John Wayne on the set of his classic 1953 film *Hondo*.

PHOTO CREDITS

JAMES ELLIS is a writer and former editor of *The Official John Wayne Collector's Edition* magazine, a celebration of the life and legacy of one of America's greatest icons. Ellis is also the author of *The Official John Wayne Handy Book for Men* and the editor of the special edition *Men's Health: Ultimate Guide to Everything*.

Media Lab Books
For inquiries, call 646-449-8614

Copyright 2023 Topix Media Lab

Published by Topix Media Lab
14 Wall Street, Suite 3C
New York, NY 10005

Printed in Korea

ISBN-13: 978-1-956403-16-9
ISBN-10: 1-956403-16-7

CEO Tony Romando

Vice President & Publisher Phil Sexton
Senior Vice President of Sales & New Markets Tom Mifsud
Vice President of Retail Sales & Logistics Linda Greenblatt
Chief Financial Officer Vandana Patel
Manufacturing Director Nancy Puskuldjian
Digital Marketing & Strategy Manager Elyse Gregov

Chief Content Officer Jeff Ashworth
Director of Editorial Operations Courtney Kerrigan
Senior Acquisitions Editor Noreen Henson
Creative Director Susan Dazzo
Photo Director Dave Weiss
Executive Editor Tim Baker

Content Editor Juliana Sharaf
Content Designer Glen Karpowich
Features Editor Trevor Courneen
Assistant Managing Editor Tara Sherman
Designer Mikio Sakai
Copy Editor & Fact Checker Madeline Raynor
Junior Designer Alyssa Bredin Quirós
Assistant Photo Editor Jenna Addesso

Cover Illustration by Richard Phipps. Photo Reference: Collection Christophel/Alamy

Topix Media Lab would like to thank John Wayne Enterprises, custodian of the John Wayne Archives, for providing unfettered access to their private and personal collection. Best efforts were made by Topix Media Lab to find and credit the photographers.

Topix Media Lab makes no specific claim of ownership of images contained in this publication and is claiming no specific copyright to images used. The mission of the John Wayne Cancer Foundation is to bring courage, strength and grit to the fight against cancer. *johnwayne.org*